A Simplistic Approach to Macroeconomics

Rodolfo Rivas

Miami Dade Community College

I would like to thank Devry University and Keller Graduate Center's for allowing me to be part of their teams.
Cordially,
R. Rivas

KENDALL/HUNT PUBLISHING COMPANY
4050 Westmark Drive Dubuque, Iowa 52002

ISBN 0-7575-1358-1

Printed in the United States of America
10 9 8 7 6 5 4 3 2 1

Dedication

To the jewels of my treasure:
Nicole and Tatiana; also, to the reliable Nelly.

Contents

Preface *vii*

Part I

1. Economics and the World Around Us 3
2. Individual Markets and the Market Process 13
3. Private and Public Sectors in our Economy 29

Part II

4. Macroeconomic Measurements 39
5. Business Cycle, Unemployment, and Inflation 47
6. Macroeconomic Equilibrium Point, Aggregate Demand, and Aggregate Supply 53
7. Aggregate Spending 57

Part III

8. Money and the Banking System 63
9. Monetary Policy 65
10. International Trade 67

Part IV

Economic Articles 69

Part V

Economic Articles 87

Part VI

Economic Articles 107

Glossary *125*

Preface

The overall purpose of this workbook is to reinforce the economic principles and concepts found in the macroeconomic aspects of our economy. Semester after semester, students have expressed their interest in a simpler , concise, and updated workbook that deciphers how the macroeconomic aspects of the economy works. This workbook is in response to that interest.

PART I

CHAPTER

1

Economics and the World Around Us

"The mere formulation of a problem is far more essential than its solution, which may merely be a matter of mathematical or experimental skill. To raise new questions, new possibilities, to regard old problems from a new angle requires creative imagination and marks real advances in science."

—Albert Einstein

Throughout history, societies have strived to cope with the dilemma of having limited resources—land, labor, capital, entrepreneurial ability, which after transforming into output (goods and services) are called factors of production—to satisfy the society's desires. Those wants, have been different from century to century and from decade to decade, and are different from county to county, from region to region, and from city to city. Society's members (people) have managed to provide some type of remedy to compensate for this imbalance between limited resources and desires, by increasing output (goods and services) given the available limited resources and the available level of technology (ongoing changing factors). Every society confronts this dilemma of scarcity, and must somehow answer the basic questions:

- What are the goods and services to be produced?
- How are the goods and services to be produced?
- For whom are the goods and services to be produced?

We answer these questions using our rational behavior (self-interest) and our marginal analysis (Marginal Benefit = Marginal Cost) to come up with our optimal choice, which is reached by any household, business, or government agency. There is a trade-off taking place when we use this marginal analysis at any level in our economy; choosing to produce one item, good, or service means choosing not to produce something else. We economists illustrate these trade-offs by drawing a production possibility curve. This curve illustrates the concepts of scarcity and opportunity cost and shows all the possible combinations of goods and services a society could produce.

The production possibility curve appears bowed out from the point of origin (0,0)—the first quadrant of the coordinate system—because of the law of increasing opportunity costs. To an economist, this cost is measured by obtaining the best alternative opportunity forgone when choosing a course of action. This implies that a nation is limited to the combination of output (goods and services) shown by its production possibility domestically. However, specialization and trade can move or expand this level of output (goods and services) to another level or frontier. In the study of the economy, we break economics into two categories: microeconomics and macroeconomics Microeconomics looks at the behavior of individuals, businesses, and government agencies. On the other hand, macroeconomics deals with the entire economy. It should be noted that economics is a "social science," which is not exact, and that is what makes this "social science" so interesting.

Learning Objectives

After reading chapters 1 and 2 and doing the following exercises, you should:

- Know that economics is the study of how to allocate society's resources—land, labor, capital, and limited entrepreneurship.
- Know that scarcity results because limited resources are not sufficient to satisfy all of society's desires and wants.
- Be able to know and illustrate opportunity cost, using production possibilities curves.
- Understand the law of increasing opportunity costs—no such thing as a "free lunch."
- Be able to illustrate efficiency, growth, unemployment, and underemployment, using production possibilities curve.
- Know the basic questions—what, how, for whom?
- Distinguish between microeconomics vs. macroeconomics.
- Be able to discuss tradeoffs.

Definitions

Social science

Economics

Scarcity

Choice

Tradeoffs

Rational behavior

Ceteris paribus

Self-interest

Marginal

Marginal analysis

Questions

1. What is economics and why is it important?
2. What is "scarcity" and how does it affect you?
3. Explain self-interest and how the marginal works.
4. Explain what the production possibilities curve illustrates:

Name: ______________________ Date: ______________

PUZZLE I

Using Key Terms

Fill in the puzzle on this page by matching the concepts to the following information found under "across" and "down" areas.

Across

1. There is no such thing as a "free lunch."
3. Happens when government intervention fails to improve economic outcomes.
6. The transformation of land, labor, capital, and entrepreneurship into goods and services.
7. Branch of economics concerned with the behavior of individuals, firms, and government agencies.
11. The study of how best to allocate society's limited resources.
16. Latin meaning for "other things equal."
17. Economic policy supported by Adam Smith (1776).

Down

2. The curve which illustrated the tradeoffs, scarcity, law of opportunity cost.
4. The limited resources used to come up with a new or a better product.
5. The study of the overall economy.
8. The use of market signals and government directives to select the mix of output.
10. Happens when the market mechanism produces wrong mix of output.
12. Final goods utilized for producing other goods.
13. Imbalance between limited resources and society's desires.
15. The increase of output as a result of better procedures.

Name: ______________________ Date: ______________

Problems and Applications

Exercise 1

Graphs

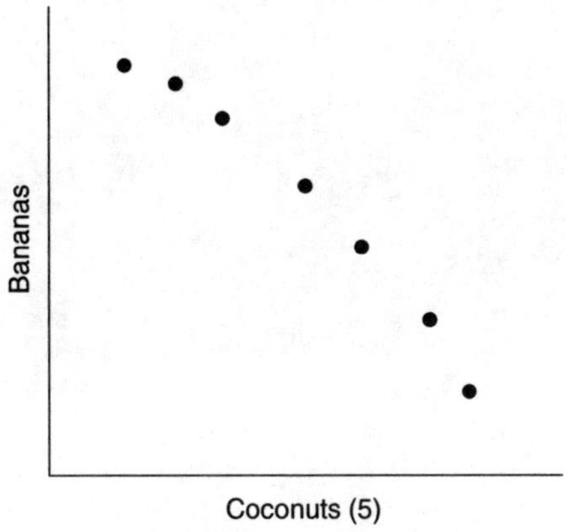

1. Tradeoffs occurs because of ________________.
2. Producing more coconut means ________________.
3. As the production of coconuts increases, ________________.
4. As the production of bananas increases, ________________.

Exercise 2

Graph B

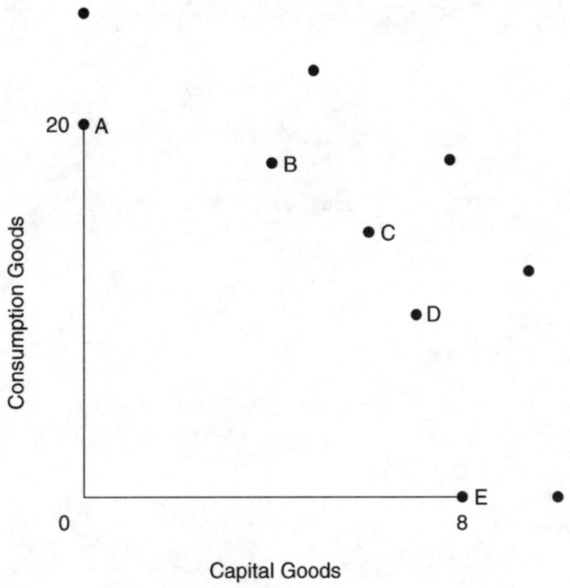

1. Economic growth occurs ________________.
2. At what point will economic growth be the fastest?
3. Why?

Name: ____________________ Date: ____________

Exercise 3

Suppose you have only 20 hours per week to study. The following table shows the tradeoff between leisure time (not studying) and the grade point average achieved as a result of studying.

	a	b	c	d	e
Leisure Time (hours/week)	20	18	15	10	0
Grade Point Average	0	1	2	3	4

1. Draw production possibility
2. What is the opportunity cost of raising your grade point average from 2.0 to 3.0? from 3.0 to 4.0? What are the tradeoffs?

Exercise 4

Graph C

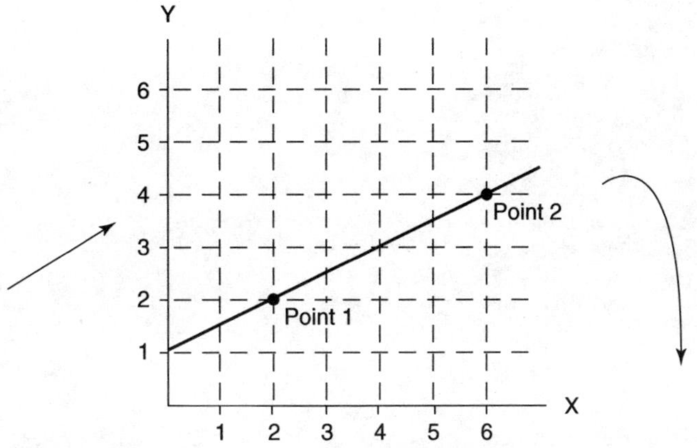

1. The vertical distance between the two points equals ____________________.
2. The horizontal distance between the two point equals ____________________.
3. The slope of the line equals ____________________.
4. The slope the line is (positive/negative) ____________________

CHAPTER

2

Individual Markets and the Market Process

"Teach a parrot to say supply and demand and you have an economist!"

—Unknown

Previously, we exposed ourselves to a brief taste of some the basic fundamentals of economics and the world around us. In this chapter, we are going to understand how a market economy creates the essential features of the market-directed activity: demand and supply. This market-directed activity tries to answer some fundamental questions:

- What determines the price of a good or a service?
- How does the price of a product affect its production/consumption?
- Why do prices often change?

But, who are the participants? How do they interact? Why do they behave in that way? In one plane, we find the households (also known as spenders, consumers, buyers). This group of humans will look into purchasing goods and services by maximizing their purchasing power with relation to their disposable income (income after taxes). Therefore, the prices of these goods and services will be the key determinant for the level of quantity purchased. Economists illustrate this relationship between price and quantity purchased in the form of the **demand curve** or **demand schedule.** Therefore, the quantity demanded of products and services in a market is the quantity that buyers are willing and able to buy at any particular price.

When prices fall, households (consumers, buyers) will increase quantity demanded (purchase more goods and services). This interaction between Prices__ ↑ up,__ ↓ down then QD, (quantity demanded) ↓ down, ↑ up is called the **law of demand.**

$$P\uparrow \ QD\downarrow$$
$$P\downarrow \ QD\uparrow$$

This interaction creates an inverse relationship between prices and quantity demanded. Households are concerned about getting the best deal possible. So, demand is the ability and willingness to buy quantities of goods or services at alternative prices in a given time frame, while, of course, keeping everything also constant *(ceteris paribus)*.

All these movements are along the demand curve. When we look at total shift of the demand curve to the right or to the left, the shift factors are presented. In this area, we have the prices of substitutes, prices of complements (when the good is normal), income (when the good is inferior), population, consumer expectations of future price, tastes, and preferences. These factors will have an impact on the shift of the demand curve to the right or left.

Now, let's look at the other participant in this market's interaction. We find the suppliers, also known as the sellers, the vendors, or the businesses. Here, we deal with a different process from the one presented previously by the demander. Here, we find that the quantity supplied of goods and services in a market is the quantity the sellers, vendors, or businesses are willing and able to sell at any particular price. When prices rise, the quantity supplied increases. Suppliers want to be profitable. Therefore, when price goes up, QS(quantity supplied) goes up. This is called the law of supply.

Economists illustrate this direct relationship (a positive slope) between prices and the quantity supplied in a **supply schedule,** also known as the **supply curve.** So, **supply** is the ability and willingness to sell specific quantities of a good or a service at alternative prices in a given time frame, keeping everything constant *(ceteris paribus)*.

The total shift of the supply curve to right or to left is induced by the **determinants of supply.** These determinants are the number of buyers, the price of labor or other inputs, production restriction, technology, prices of substitutes in production, prices of jointly produced products, and Producer expectations of future prices.

These curves interact with the goal to find the equilibrium price and the rate of production of goods or services in a market (interaction between buyer and seller). These curves can represent the interaction of one individual or several.

When demand curve intersects the supply curve, the market is in equilibrium (price equilibrium and Q supplied = Q demanded).

If the market price is above the equilibrium price, a surplus appears. When quantity supplied (QS) is more than actual quantity demanded (QD < QS), the seller lowers prices and production rates. Buyers purchase more at these lower prices (law of demand) and we get back to the QD = QS. On the other hand, when the market price is below the equilibrium price, a shortage appear. Quantity demanded (QD) is more than actual quantity supplied. Buyers bid up the prices and sellers increase production rates (QD > QS).

Learning Objectives

- Understand the basis questions in economics and how the U.S. economy answers the questions.
- Be able to describe the different types of markets and the motivations of participants in those markets.
- Be familiar with how a demand schedule represents demand and how a supply schedule represents supply.
- Be able to graph supply and demand curves.
- Understand why supply and demand curves shift.
- Understand what causes movements along demand and supply curves.
- Know the difference between individual demand and supply vs. market demand and market supply.
- Explain shortages and surpluses and the effects of price ceilings and price floors.
- Describe how and why markets move toward equilibrium.

Name: ______________________________ Date: ______________

PUZZLE II

Using Key Terms

Fill in the puzzle on this page with the appropriate term from the list of Key Terms at the end of the chapter in the text.

Across

3. The result of rent controls creates a market.
6. Changes from $2.00 to $3.00 to reach equilibrium.
7. To sell various quantities of a good at alternative prices.
10. To buy a particular good at some price.
12. The assumption that nothing else changes.(term)
15. Businesses purchase the factors of production.
16. The use of market price and sales to produce desired output.
17. The inverse relationship between price and quantity.

Down

1. The result of an income change.
2. When consumers go to the internet and place their bid (for instance, price line.com web page).
3. When the sum of all business sales intentions comes short.
4. The name of all demand curves.
5. Goods and services are exchanges in Qs>Qd implies ______.
8. Quantity supplied is greater than Quantity demanded.
9. The response when we have some local governments, including New York City and San Francisco, to place control in rent prices.
11. Explains why the curve in supply has a positive slope.
13. When we give up something, in order to get something else.
14. After adding all demand curves.

Name: ______________________ Date: ______________

The Demand Curve—Principles and Development

Demand is: ______________________

A Demand Schedule is: ______________________

A Demand Curve is: ______________________

Price	Quantity Demanded

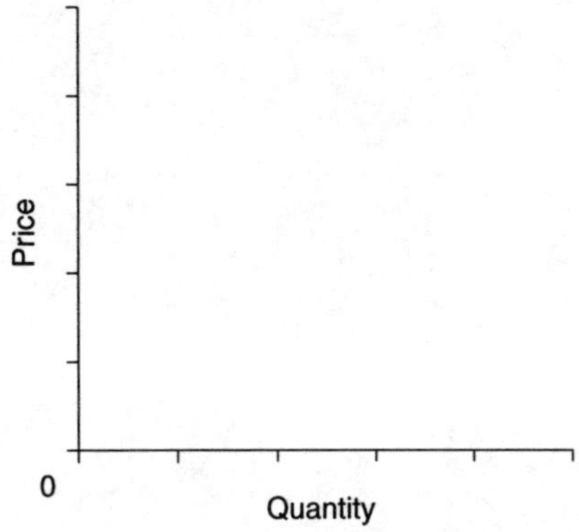

Demand is: ______________________

____

Quantity Demanded is: ______________________

____

Price-Quantity relationship: ______________________

____

The "Law of Demand" states: ______________________

____

Determinants of Demand: ______________________

____

____

____

____

____

____

Name: ______________________ Date: ______________

The Demand Curve—Increase in Demand

An *increase* in Demand is: ______________________

____

____

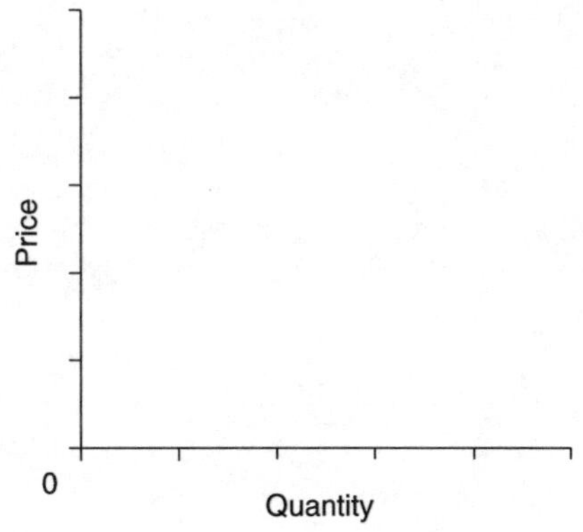

Things that increase Demand:

____

____

____

____

____

____

____

____

____

____

____

____

Name: ______________________ Date: ______________

The Demand Curve—Decrease in Demand

A *Decrease* in Demand is: ______________________

____

____

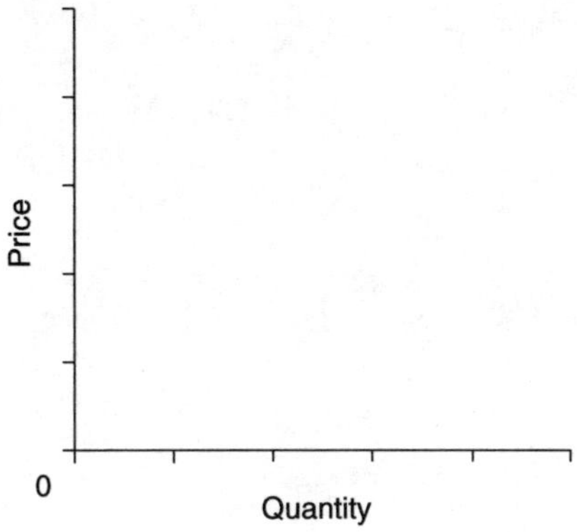

Things that decrease Demand:

____

____

____

____

____

____

____

____

____

____

____

____

Name: ______________________________ Date: ______________

The Supply Curve—Principles and Development

Supply is: ______________________________

A Supply Schedule is: ______________________________

A Supply Curve is: ______________________________

Price	Quantity ~~Demanded~~ SUPPLIED

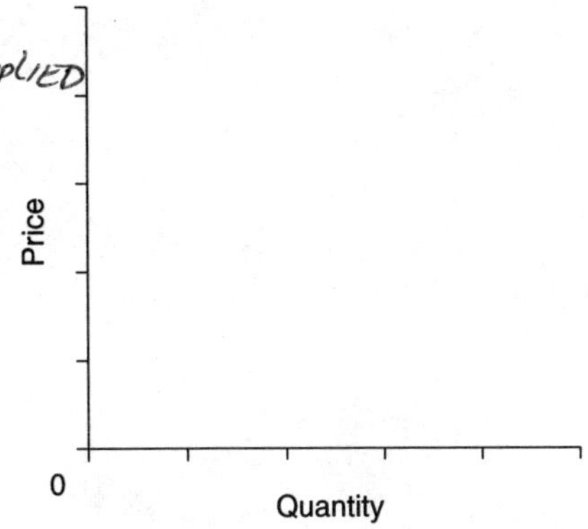

Supply is: ______________________________

____

Quantity Supplied is: ______________________________

____

Price-Quantity relationship: ______________________________

____

The "Law of Supply" states: ______________________________

____

Determinants of Supply: ______________________________

____

____

____

____

____

____

Name: ______________________ Date: ____________

The Supply Curve—Increase in Supply

An *increase* in Supply is:______________________

____

____

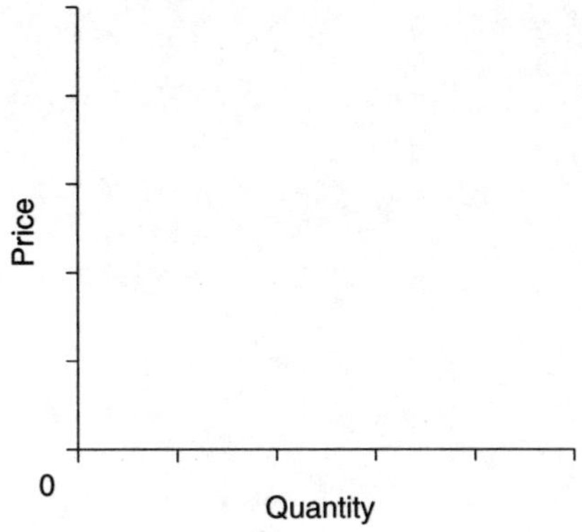

Things that increase Supply:

____

____

____

____

____

____

____

____

____

____

____

____

Name: ______________________ Date: ______________

The Supply Curve—Decrease in Supply

A *decrease* in Supply is: ______________________

____

____

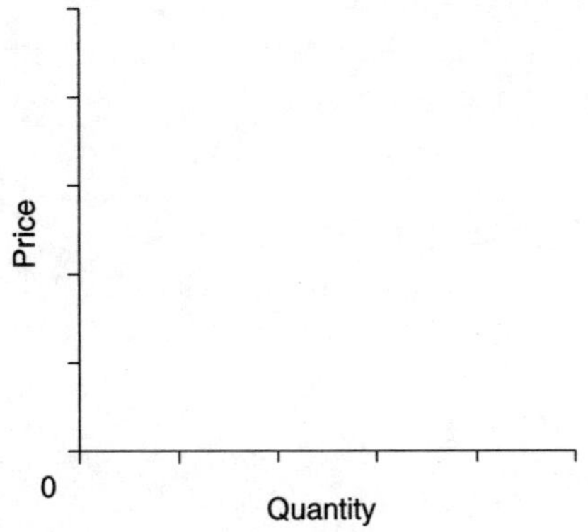

Things that decrease Supply:

____

____

____

____

____

____

____

____

____

____

____

____

CHAPTER

3

Private and Public Sectors in our Economy

"I am not friend to a very energetic government. It is always oppressive."

—Thomas Jefferson

The combined levels of private sector—households, business—and the combined levels of public sector—federal, state, and local—have a major impact on answering the questions of what to produce, how to produce, and for whom to produce in the U.S. economy or any other economy throughout the world. In this chapter, we explore some questions;

- Do we really need a public sector?
- What output (goods/services) are supposed to be produced by the public sector?
- How much participation does the public sector need to have in the economy?

During the Great Depression, we faced a major failure in the interaction between prices and sales (market mechanism), which, of course, led to many market failures. We justify the existence of the public sector because of the inability of the private sector to provide the optimal mix of output (goods/services) to the current needs and wants created by our society. When we examine the private sector more closely, we find the two key players (households, businesses) interacting and creating the **consumption relationship** (consumption expenditures and disposable income). Households will demand output (goods/services); these outputs fall under the categories of durable goods (expected lives of three years or more), non-durable goods (expected lives of less than three years), and services.

As we speak, two thirds of goods/services are consumed in our economy, representing the C (consumption expenditures) variable found in the GDP (gross domestic product) equation. Businesses are the second player. Businesses have different legal forms: sole proprietor, partnerships (two or more), or corporations (legal entities).

Now, we know that the public sector is present when there is a market failure created by the interaction of the players found in the private sector. Therefore, the public sector steps in and offers other alternatives that the private sector can't provide. These alternatives are in the form of public goods, for example, national defense (Homeland Security as a consequence of 9/11 tragedy). Some of these goods and services are consumed jointly, by those who pay and by those who don't. The ones who don't pay are called "free riders." Public goods don't possess the exclusion principle; private goods do possess the exclusion principle. Another reasons for having the public sector interacting in our economy is the existence of **externalities**—benefits or costs of a market activity that are borne by a third party. Externalities can be negative (pollution from a factory). The public sector intervenes to correct these negative externalities (new legislation laws). The existence of market power - the ability of a single firm to alter the market price of any product or service - also justifies public sector intervention. Consequently, competition is a basic mechanism to foster a healthy market system.

The public sector also provides assistance in the forms of federal expenditures on goods and services, transfer of payments (unemployment benefits, food stamps), interest on the public debt, and general aid to state and local governments, all supported by the federal personal income taxes, social security taxes, corporate income taxes, excise taxes, and other taxes.

When we deal with these market failures (micro level) we are on the production possibilities curve. Macro failures can also occur in such even, we fail to reach the desirable level in the production possibilities curve.

Learning Objectives

- Be able to understand how macro failure justifies public-sector activity.
- Be able to recognize the opportunity costs of public-sector activity.
- Be able to know how the mechanism of public decision-making differs form the market mechanism.
- Be able to know the effects of externalities and how they are handled in the economy.
- Understand the essentials of public choice.

Definitions

Public sector

Private sector

Public good

Private good

Free-rider person

Market mechanism

Public choice

Antitrust laws

Monopoly

Categorical grants

Name: ______________________ Date: ______________

PUZZLE III

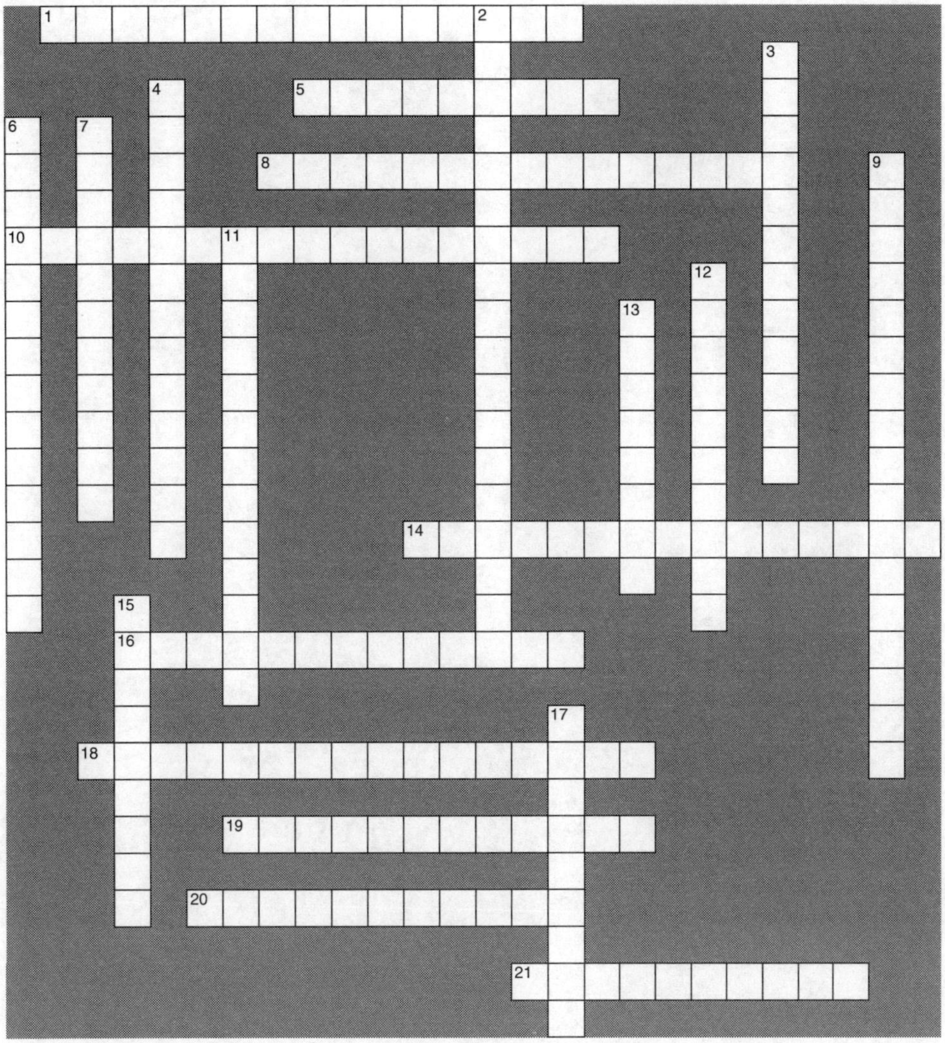

Using Key Terms

Across

1. The desired goods and services that are given up in order to obtain something else.
5. An increase in the average price level.
8. Known as the "invisible hand."
10. When the outcome of government intervention is not the one expected.
14. An industry controlled by a single firm.
16. What type of tax illustrates the inverse relationship between income and taxes.
18. When government is addressing the FOR WHOM question.
19. The role of self-interest in public decision-making.
20. When a single firm has the ability to alter the market price.
21. The fee paid for using a public sector good or service.

Down

2. When we produce the ideal level of output.
3. Happens when people are willing to work but are unable to find jobs.
4. The benefit or cost incurred by a third party as a consequence of a market transaction.
6. A tax which increases as long as income increases.
7. The good which has the exclusion principle.
9. Federal grants provided to state and local levels for specific purposes.
11. When the market system is not providing the desired level of output.
12. A good which can be consumed jointly.
13. Only one firm in the industry.
15. Someone who doesn't pay a bill still gets the benefit.
17. The legislation to prevent or to break up concentration of market power such as Microsoft.

Name: ____________________ Date: ____________

Problems and Applications

Exercise 1

Determine which letter best represents the following situations:

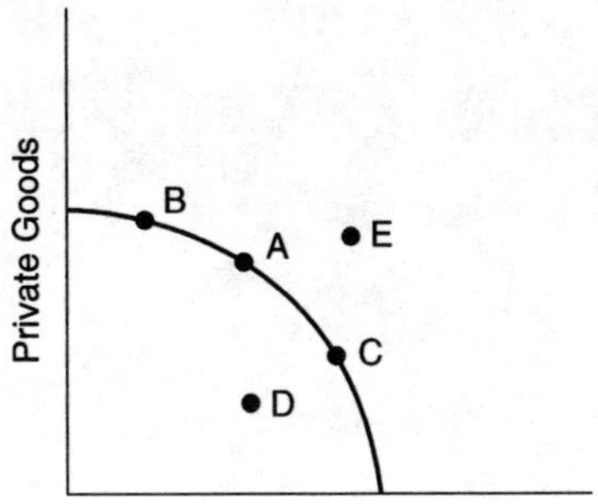

____1. Government produces more than the desired level of public goods.
____2. The free-rider person.
____3. Macro failure in the market system.
____4. When we deal with the production possibilities curve, ———— failures imply that society is at the wrong points on this curve and ———— failures imply that society is inside the curve.

PART II

CHAPTER

4

Macroeconomic Measurements

"The significant problems we face cannot be solved at the same level of thinking we were at when we created them."

—Albert Einstein

The Great Depression made of us aware of the need for having performance measurements that could indicate or provide information about the health of the economy. This unprecedented need led to the birth of the National Income Accounting System. Economist Simon Kuznets, who later became a Nobel Prize winner for this work, took over this task in conjunction with the Department of Commerce.

National Income Accounting allows to add together all the production of goods and services, using a dollar value as a common denominator. In this way, we facilitate the answers for such questions as: How much output is being produced? What is it being used for? How much income is being generated in the marketplace? During the early years of the National Income Accounting, the Gross National Product (GNP) was the measurement commonly used. Later, the Gross Domestic Product (GDP)—the total market value of all final goods and services produced within a nation's borders during a particular time frame (a quarter or a year)—took over this measurement process with more frequency.

The GDP does not include all transactions taking place in our economy. One example of these goods is the intermediate good used to produce other goods (final goods). If we were to include these goods, double counting would be created. In addition, the services of homemakers, bartering, and illegal transactions are not part of the GDP. Consequently, only new, legal, final goods and services are included in the GPD.

The GPD works as an excellent tool for comparing different economies and the changes in the output level in a single economy over time. And it can be seen as the total expenditure (GDP = C + I + G + Xn = output), the total income (wages, salaries, rent, interest, proprietor's income, corporate profits), or finally the total value added to reach the final goods and services.

The net domestic product (NDP) is derived from the GDP when we subtract the depreciation (consumption of fixed capital). In this way, we have a better measure of the changes in the production possibilities of the economy. When indirect business taxes and foreign factor income are deducted from NDP, we get the National Income. Then, to find out how much income is actually earned, we calculate personal income and disposable income, which indicates how much income is available to be spent after personal taxes are taken out.

Because the prices of goods and services change throughout the course of any time frame in any economy, and also because our standard of living is based on real goods and services, we need to accentuate the distinction between Real GDP and Nominal GDP. In order to come up with more accurate information, we need to remove the inflation from the Nominal GDP by dividing the Nominal GDP by the GDP price index (Nominal GDP/Real GDP).

In addition, we have the Consumer Price Index (CPI, a market basket made of 300 goods/services, which measures the increases/decreases in prices paid by households). We also have three Producer Price Indexes (PPI), which show the same function from the business side.

Learning Objectives

- Be able to know the purpose of national-income accounting.
- Be able to know what the GDP is made of and used for.
- Distinguish between GDP, GNP, and NDP.
- Know what is included in the GDP.
- Distinguish between Real GDP and Nominal GDP.
- Be familiar with CPI index, GDP price index, and PPI indexes.

Definitions

National Income Accounting

Gross Domestic Product

~~National~~ Net Domestic Product

Real GDP

Nominal GDP

Value added

Intermediate good

Final good

Gross investment

Net investment

Disposable income

Consumption

Saving

Depreciation

Name: ______________________ Date: ______________

PUZZLE IV

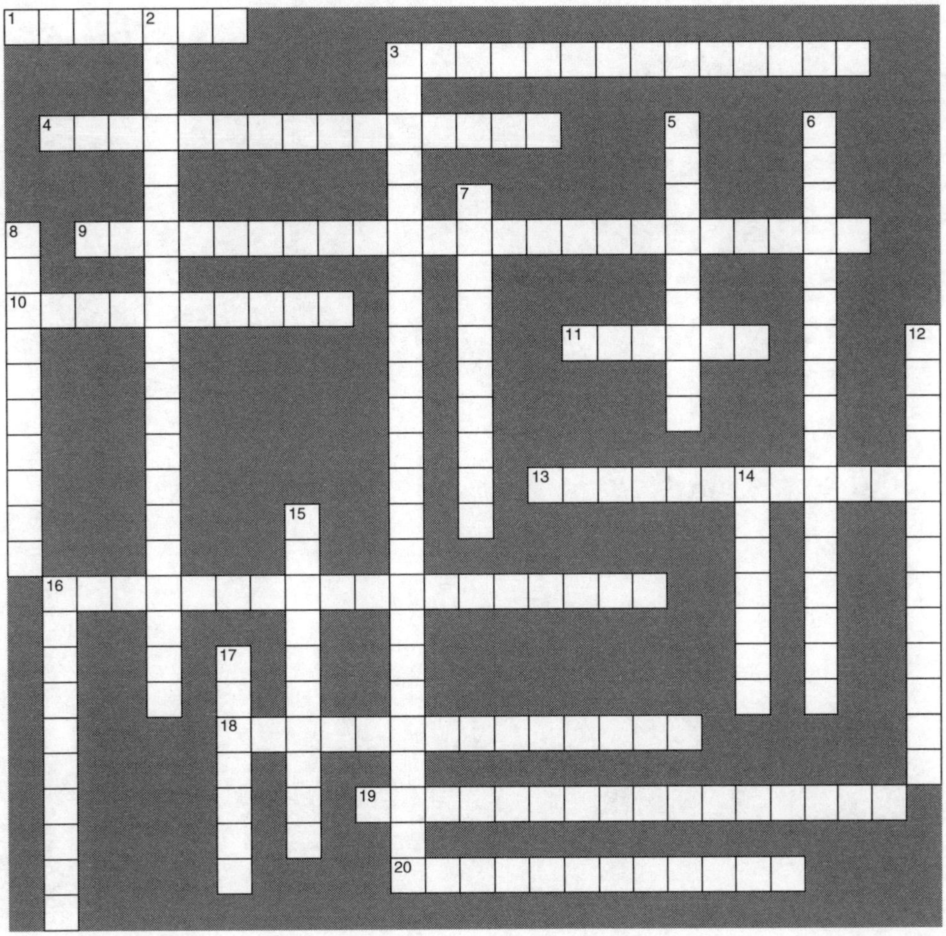

Using Key Terms

Across

1. Nominal GDP divided by GDP price index.
3. GDP minus depreciation and indirect business taxes.
4. Total investment, including depreciation.
9. Different combinations of goods and services that can be produced with available resources and technology.
10. When you add another item for the production process of a final good.
11. Disposable income minus consumption.
13. When plant and equipment wear down.
16. GDP minus depreciation.
18. Income before taxes.
19. Income after taxes.
20. GDP divided by population.

Down

2. Total of final goods and services during a time frame.
3. The measurement of an economy's total performance (aggregate activity).
5. Increase in price level.
6. Good purchased for the production of final goods.
7. The GDP not adjusted to inflation.
8. Expansion in the creation of new equipment, plants, or any human-made tools.
12. Gross investment minus depreciation.
14. The purchases of goods and services by other countries.
15. The basis for a price index.
16. Exports minus imports.
17. Goods and services to other countries.

Name: ______________________ Date: ______________

Problems and Applications

Exercise 1

Assume that orange production involves the following steps:

Step 1: A orange juice company grows its own to reduce costs.

Step 2: The orange juice company sells its orange juice to the grocery store for $1.90

Step 3: The grocery store sells its orange juice to their customers for $3.50

Find the valued added from step 1 to step 2.________

Find the valued added from step 2 to step 3.________

The orange juice sold to the store is a(an) (intermediate, final) good.

Exercise 2

	Nominal GDP	Price Index	Real GDP
Year 1	$3,500	100	
Year 2	$3,800	106	
Year 3	$4,020	112	

1. Find the real GDP for the three years.
2. The best measurement of physical changes in output is ______________.
3. According to this table, which year has the highest output level?

Exercise 3

National Income Account	Subtract items	Add items
GDP	Depreciation	
	Indirect business taxes	Transfer payments
NDP	Corporate taxes, Retained	Net interest
NI	earnings, Social Security	
PI	Taxes	
DI	Personal income taxes	
Saving	Consumption	

Use the following data to come up with the National Income Account found in the left side.

CHAPTER

5

Business Cycle, Unemployment, and Inflation

"A recession is when your neighbor loses his job. A depression is when you lose your job."

—Anonymous

The essence of macroeconomics relies on the ability to identify the contractions and expansions that the economy goes through, which directly are reflected in the total nation's output (GDP). The Great Depression of 1930s created a sense of urgency for keeping track of these contractions and expansions in the Growth Domestic Product (GDP), known as the Business Cycle. These business cycles go through four different stages, from peak to trough by watching cyclical fluctuations in the Real GDP. These business cycles vary greatly in length, frequency, and intensity. When we have two consecutive quarters of declines in Real GDP, we deal with a **recession** (contractions of Real GDP, are associated with less output and less employment). If a recession goes beyond two quarters, a **depression** originates. To tackle this slowdown in the economy, economic policies (fiscal/monetary) are utilized to induce a change in speed of the economic growth. It is essential to visualize the macroeconomic fluctuations in terms of outcomes, which depend directly on internal factors (population, innovation, corporate scandals, spending behavior), external shocks (war, terrorism, weather conditions, trade disruptions), and policies (fiscal/monetary). During these macroeconomic fluctuations in the level of output, labor changes (employment/unemployment) are present. To measure the impact on these changes in output and in labor, we need to define who is eligible and available to work (labor force). The **labor force** consists of persons eligible (16 years of age or older), currently working or full time actively seeking employment. These conditions allow us to distinguish the people given up (discouraged workers), the ones working hours less than the regular full load (part-time), and those who get jobs not using their skills completely (underemployment).

These groups contribute to obtain better data, compiled by the U.S. Bureau of Labor Statistics, to come up with the unemployment rate (unemployment × 100/labor force) and to formulate the different types of unemployment. When we deal with this side of the economy, we find frictional unemployment (short-term unemployment between jobs), seasonal unemployment (varies with the business season), structural unemployment (caused by mismatch of skills), and cyclical unemployment (created by the deficiency in aggregate demand). This last type of unemployment (cyclical) takes us away from the natural rate of unemployment (full employment level), which is reached at 5 percent. (Only frictional and structural unemployment are found.)

When we are not at that acceptable level (full employment) we have less output and we have a deficiency in the overall (aggregate) demand, leading to a gap between actual GDP and the potential GDP (obtained at 5% of full employment/unemployment rate). Aachen's law illustrates this relationship between changes in the rate of unemployment and output (Real GDP). This law (2% of output for each 1% up of the acceptable unemployment rate) is attributed to Arthur Okun, chair of the Council of Economic Advisors under President Johnson.

Learning Objectives

- Understand the importance of the business cycle.
- Have a better idea of business cycles since the Great Depression.
- Understand why aggregate demand and aggregate supply curves have that shape.
- Understand the macroeconomic equilibrium and what happens when we don't reach that level.
- Be familiar with macroeconomic problems, unemployment, and types.

Definitions

Business Cycle

Peak

Trough

Contraction

Recession

Expansion

Recovery

Unemployment rate

Labor force

Frictional unemployment

Structural unemployment

Cyclical unemployment

Discouraged worker

Natural rate of unemployment

Name: ______________________ Date: ______________

Problems and Applications

Exercise 1

Place corresponding names to the following graph label axis and cycles.

Graph (Business Cycle)

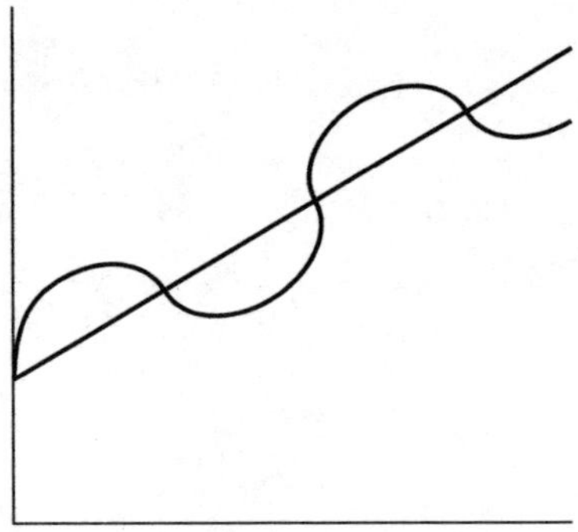

Questions

1. If business cycles are inevitable, what is the purpose of keeping track of different stages?
2. The stock market crash of October 1987 reduced the wealth of the average American household. How did this event impact the aggregate demand?

CHAPTER

6

Macroeconomic Equilibrium Point, Aggregate Demand, and Aggregate Supply

"The world is not ending."

—New York Mayor Rudy Giuliani after September 11 Terrorist Attack

When the framework for macroeconomic analysis is presented to us as a set of outcomes—output, prices growth, economic growth, and international balances—we economists combine these insights, with the use of **aggregate demand** and **aggregate supply** curves.

The first curve (the aggregate demand) slopes downward to the right, as the demand curve does. However, the aggregate demand curve downward shape is attributed to the real-balance effect, the foreign trade effect, and the interest rate effect. The aggregate demand is the total output demanded at any particular price level (GDP price index or GDP deflator), by members of the economy (households, businesses, government agencies), at any time frame. The aggregate demand encompasses the totals of consumption expenditure, investment, government, and net export. Now, when we look into the ones (businesses, government agencies) provide this output, we step into the aggregate supply curve. The aggregate supply curve has a positive slope that moves gently upward. Higher prices provide incentives to sell more output. This level of real output is obtained where aggregate demand (AD) cuts the aggregate supply curve (AS). This aggregate supply curve has different ranges: horizontal range (deficiency of AD), intermediate range (where the full employment level is obtained), and vertical range (price level's growth—demand pulls inflation level).

The macro equilibrium level of the economy is obtained in the short run at the interception point of these AD=AS curves in the intermediate range of the aggregate supply curve, with acceptable price levels, with the full employment level (5% natural rate of unemployment), and with the ideal potential GDP. In the long run, the aggregate supply (AS) curve turns vertical because the cost structure follows output prices.

In recent years, we experienced important interactions of these AD/AS macroeconomic framework analysis. During the mid-1960s, the rapid outward shift in the aggregate demand moved up beyond the macro equilibrium point to the vertical range of the aggregate supply line, leading to higher prices (demand-pull inflation). In the 1970s, we had a number of adverse supply shocks (food/oil industries), inducing an upward movement in the aggregate supply (AS) curve, leading to less output and higher prices (cost-push inflation). In early 2000s, we have been exposed to a deficiency of aggregate demand (AD), which is found in the horizontal range of the aggregate supply (AS) curve, bringing a high level of unemployment, moving us away from reaching the potential GDP level.

Learning Objectives

- Understand what the significance of the Aggregate Demand & Aggregate Supply framework.
- Why the Aggregate Demand & Aggregate Supply curves have that shape.
- Be familiar with the different ranges found in the Aggreagate Supply curve.
- Distinguish between Demand-Pull inflation & Cost-push inflation.

Definitions

Aggregate demand

Aggregate supply

Real-balance effect

Interest rate effect

Foreign trade effect

GDP price index

Consumption expenditure

Investment

Net export

Acceptable macro equilibrium point

Name: ______________________ Date: ______________

Problem and Application

Exercise 1

Place corresponding names to the following graph.

Graph (AS/AS Framework)

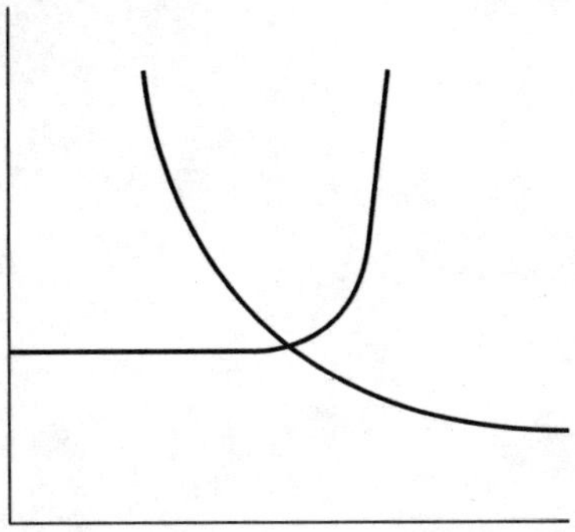

Questions

1. What is the reasons for the AD curve to have the downward shape?
2. How can an economy eliminate cyclical unemployment?

CHAPTER

7

Aggregate Spending

"I place the economy among the first and most important virtues, and public debt as the greatest of dangers."

—Thomas Jefferson

A new way of thought about economics was created after the Great Depression. One major contributor to this new way of thought about economies was John Maynard Keynes. He concluded that the market-driven economy was unstable, and could fall into an undefined recessionary trap (as in fact happened). Furthermore, he insisted that to get out of that recessionary trap, government needed to play an active role for promoting investment from the public or private sectors, by using fiscal and monetary policies.

Keynes mentioned that the demand side aggregate demand (AD curve) of the economy could not have sufficient "ammunition" to shift on its own and to generate the desired full employment level. After completion of his work, he came up with the conclusion that the consumption expenditure sector (durable goods, non-durables, and services) was and still is the most important element in the total spending process, and is primarily determined by the available disposable income level (personal income minus taxes). In addition, the available disposable income can be used in two different ways: to be consumed or to be saved. This level of disposable income can be anticipated by using the Consumption function (Keynes's invention):

$$© = a + b\ yd$$

(where *yd* = personal – taxes), *c* stands for consumption expenditures, *a* stands for autonomous spending (wealth, credit, age, taxes) and *b* % of current disposable income spent (MPC).

If we (people) were to spend all our available disposable income, we would have a perfectly even 45-degree angle line with a function of C = DI, which illustrates the relationship between consumption expenditure and disposable income, and we find that actual investments equal planned investment. We also find a perfect, smooth circular flow between the households (disposable income) and businesses (goods and services). However, we find that this smooth circular flow doesn't hold forever, because we (people) tend to save, and that less income available the level of saving depends on the level of disposable income. This is illustrated by the fraction of disposable income (Average Propensity to consume APC = Consumption/Income.

In addition, savings, imports, and taxes are leakages that affect this circular flow, creating changes that directly affect the consumption and disposable levels. This is defined by what is called MPC (Marginal Propensity to Consume): change in consumption/change in income. We also have the MPS (Marginal Propensity to Save), which corresponds to change in saving to change in income (MPS = Changes in Savings/Changes in Income). These changes produce a multiplier effect that works upward or downward, enlarging increases or decreases in investment. We economists assume that values of MPC and MPS are constant; not only is there statistical evidence, but it also simplifies economic analysis. Note that

$$MPC + MPS = 1 \text{ and } APC + APS = 1.$$

Learning Objectives

- Understand how a shift in consumption function leads to a shift in Aggregate Demand.
- Know that the consumption function was Mr. Keynes' invention.
- Be able to differenciate between Disposable Income, Personal Income, Savings.
- Know the differences between the average and marginal propensities to consume or to save.

Definitions

Durable goods

Non-durable goods

Services

Keynes's function

APS

APC

MPC

MPS

Multiplier effect

Questions

1. What events in the economy can contribute to the change in the consumer confidence level?
2. What are the participants of the aggregate demand curve?

PART III

CHAPTER

8

Money and the Banking System

Throughout history, the global economy has run on the trade of good and services. Humans have been able to perform business operations and transactions using some type of exchange. To fulfill our desires, we swap one good for another, or one good for a service, or a service for another good, which is known as barter.

However, to bring higher efficiency levels in the economy and to smooth business transactions, money is used as an instrument to reach those goals. Money can be used as a medium of exchange, which promotes wealth and efficient business transactions. Money provides and serves as a unit of account, providing us a yardstick, an equivalence to something that is universally understood. In addition, money can store its value, promoting the sense of holding wealth. Money changes its form into paper money and coins. Money can be distributed into three different categories: M1, M2 and M3. M1, known as the most liquid measure of money, is composed of currency (paper plus coins, traveler's checks, and other checks). M2 is the second category and includes M1, previously mentioned, plus savings (CDs), less mutual funds less than $100,000. Lastly, we have M3, which includes M1 and M2, and long-time deposits equal to or greater than $100,000.

The banking industry has different representations. We find **commercial banks,** state and national banks that provide checking and savings, CDS, loans, and insurance by FDIC up to $100,000. **Thrift institutions** offer the same range of banking services as commercial banks; they are also insured by FDIC. We also find **insurance companies, mutual fund companies, pension funds,** and **securities firms.** All of these banking entities possess some type of control of the supply of money.

Learning Objectives

- Be familiar with the basic characteristics & functions of money.
- Be familiar with the composition of the money supply (M1,M2.M3).
- Be aware of the different banking entities.

Definitions

Money

Barter

Money supply 1

Money supply 2

Money supply 3

Store

Unit of account

Medium of exchange

Store of value

CHAPTER

9

Monetary Policy

"There have been three great inventions since the beginning of time: fire, the wheel, and central banking."

—Will Rogers

As previously mentioned, any banking entity possesses some type of control of the supply of money in the economy. However, every country in the world uses a central bank system to keep the nations's economy on course. The Federal Reserve System—also known as "Fed"—is the central bank in the United States. It was created by the Glass-Owen Bill 12/23/13 (the Federal Reserve Act of 1913) with the purpose of promoting U.S. economic stability. It has 12 regional banks throughout the nation, which control the entire banking industry in the country. Federal Reserve Systems, U.S. central bank, deals with monetary policy, keeps cash deposits, and performs several other functions. It has seven boards of governors and, by adding five more members (regional presidents of federal banks), transforms itself into the Federal Open Market Committee (FOMC). This committee buys and sells of treasury bonds from/to the public, reduces or increases the bank requirements (bank reserves kept to meet Fed's reserve requirement), and reduces or increases the discount rate (interest rate imposed by the Fed banks on loans to other banks); it also affects the federal fund rate (the interest rate on loans provided by banks to other banks).

The FOMC uses these three tools (buying-selling bonds, increase-decrease discount rate, increase-decrease bank's revenue requirement), depending on the economic performance. Eased monetary policy (buy treasury bonds, decrease discount rate, decrease bank's reserve requirement) is associated with a high level of unemployment (cyclical). Tight monetary policy (sell treasury bonds, increase discount rate, increase bank's reserve requirement) is valid during inflationary periods.

Learning Objectives

- Be aware of the structure, organization, and purpose of the Federal Reserve System.
- Understand how the Open Market Committee uses different monetary policies.
- Be familiar with federal fund rate, discount rate, and bank's reserves.
- Know the difference between Federal Reserve regional banks and other banks.

Definitions

Federal Reserve System

FOMC

Regional Fed bank

Eased monetary policy

Tight monetary policy

Discount rate

Federal fund rate

Bank's reserve requirement

CHAPTER

10

International Trade

"We came over on different ships, but we're all in the same boat now."

—Dr. Martin Luther King, Jr.

Throughout the history of the world, nations have understood how important the trade of goods and services is for producing more total output (Real GDP) than they could in the absence of trade. Furthermore, all nations realize that they face the dilemma of scarcity (limited resources), and the need for allocating these limited resources in an efficient and intelligent way.

Comparative advantage (doing things least costly), **absolute advantage** (doing things best), and **specialization** cause countries to benefit from trade and to move their existing production possibilities curve to a higher level. Nations seldom are found with a **trade balance** [(X–IM)=0]. We usually expect to find either a **trade surplus** [(X–IM)>0] or a **trade deficit** [(X–IM)<0]. Even though the trade deficit permits nations to consume more goods and services than they can produce, it may complicate the effectiveness of a fiscal policy at the internal level in a nation.

Learning Objectives

- Understand the macroeconomic impact of international trade.
- Be able to differentiate between comparative and absolute advantages.
- Understand why specialization and trade increase both production possibilities and consumption possibilities.

Definitions

Comparative advantage

Absolute advantage

Export

Imports

Trade balance

Trade surplus

Trade deficit

Questions

1. If we have a strong dollar, are American firms stronger and more competitive?
2. When we have a trade deficit, are U.S. producers inefficient?

PART

IV

Economic Articles

Part IV

- Opportunities and Costs
- Increasing the Mandated Minimum Wage; Who Pays the Price?
- Marginalism and the Morality of Pricing Human Lives
- Kathie Lee's Children
- Markets and Freedom
- Socialized Medicine is the Problem
- The Problem with Price Controls
- Demand and Supply

Opportunities and Costs

Dwight Lee

Economic Notions

My previous have columns have been devoted to an overview of how markets work by facilitating social cooperation: providing people with the information and motivation to pursue their own advantages in ways that best create opportunities for others. My emphasis has been on the forest rather than the individual trees of economic understanding. Now I shall begin looking at some of the key concepts essential to applying economic reasoning to all human activity. I begin with opportunity cost.

Limits and Opportunities

Economics has been called the dismal science because it studies the most fundamental of all problems, scarcity. Because of scarcity we all face the dismal reality that there are limits to what we can do. No matter how productive we become, we can never accomplish and enjoy as much as we would like. The only thing we can do without limit is desire more. Because of scarcity, every time we do one thing we necessarily have to forgo doing something else desirable. So there is an opportunity cost to everything we do, and that cost is expressed in terms of the most valuable alternative that is sacrificed.

But the pervasiveness of costs suggests that the dismal reality of limits is only one side of a coin with a brighter side. The limits of scarcity create costs only when there are opportunities. Eliminate the opportunity to choose among alternatives and there are no costs. If, for example, I am forced to live in a particular house, take a particular job, marry a particular woman, and consume a set bundle of goods, I incur no costs when I do those things. So the bright side of costs is the opportunities that create them. Expand our opportunities and the costs of everything we do increase.

Although we commonly see cost as something to avoid, in fact we are better off living in an economy where we are forced to confront the cost of everything we do. I personality might be better off if I could consume products without having to consider their costs because I could shift them to others. But any advantage I could realize would be more than offset if others could ignore the costs of their activities and shift them to me. As a result, we would all lack the information and motivation to choose wisely. Only when the costs of choices are imposed on those who make those choices can we best use the opportunities available.

This is one way of explaining the advantage of market prices. The prices people pay in the marketplace reflect the opportunity costs of their choices. You cannot generally purchase a good or service in a free market for less than others are willing to pay for it, or for less than the amount spent to make it available, which is an important part of the social cooperation that emerges out of market transactions.

Special Interests Don't Want Costs Considered

Unfortunately, many economic decisions are made not in a market setting in response to market prices, but by government in response to political considerations. This creates opportunities for the politically influential to acquire benefits paid for by the general public. Invariably, those seeking political benefits downplay the costs in the hope of justifying larger expenditures; they commonly argue that some things are so important that costs shouldn't even be considered.

Educators argue that education is too important to be considered in terms of costs; environmentalists argue that saving the earth is so imperative that environmental programs should be implemented regardless of the costs; recipients of medical research grants argue that human health trumps any crass consideration of costs; and people supported by the National Endowment for the Arts claim that the value of "art goes to the very soul of what it means to be human! and is contaminated when compared with dollars and cents:" (That's a close paraphrase of a statement on arts funding that I heard on National Public Radio.)

All these statements are best understood as attempts by organized groups to capture more public money. To consider costs has nothing to do with exaggerating the importance of money. Money provides a convenient way of expressing costs, but money is not the cost of anything. When I put down a ten-dollar bill to pay for a meal, the money may appear to be the cost, but the real cost is the opportunity cost—the subjective value I forgo by spending the money on the meal rather than spending it on the most valuable alternative.

Silly Claims

To claim that we shouldn't consider the cost of doing some things is equivalent to claiming that we should do those things without considering the alternatives. That such a transparently silly claim continues to be used in special interest pleading illustrates the power of deception over logic in political debate. Not considering the alternatives to doing something would make sense only if it were always more valuable than anything else. But this means that we should devote all of our resources to this one thing. If it were really true that fine orchestral music, for example, was so valuable that costs shouldn't be considered, then everyone should go homeless and hungry and spend all of their time listening to orchestras in the nude. This is obviously silly, but not one but sillier than arguing that something is so important that it is inappropriate to consider its cost.

As soon as two or more groups claim that their program should be funded without considering costs, the relevance of costs should be obvious. Educating our youth and curing our sick cannot both be too important to consider cost, not in a world of scarcity. The cost of doing more to educate our youth is doing less to cure our sick, and vice versa. To ignore the cost of one is to treat the other as unworthy in comparison.

Of course, the reality of scarcity, and the opportunity costs than result, intrude into the political process despite the special-interest rhetoric disparaging considerations of cost.

Comparisons have to be made among competing alternatives, so opportunity costs are considered in the political process. Unfortunately, imperfections and biases in the political process prevent the opportunity cost of government action from being adequately considered. The result is what one should expect when alternatives are poorly considered. Waste occurs as decisions direct resources out of more valuable and into less valuable activities, and often into activities counterproductive to the stated objectives.

Market prices do not perfectly reflect opportunity costs, but one can appreciate how close they get by considering the perversities that arise because political decisions often ignore most of the costs of a policy. I shall consider this problem next month as a way of further illustrating the importance of opportunity costs in understanding economics.

Increasing the Mandated Minimum Wage: Who Pays the Price?

D. Mark Wilson

Less than six months after its last increase to $5.15 per hour, President Bill Clinton is proposing a hike of 19.4 percent that would raise the federally mandated minimum wage over the next two years to $6.15 per hour. During the past eight years, Congress has increased the mandated minimum wage four separate times. Before raising the minimum wage again, Congress must ask itself a fundamental question: Should it be illegal for Americans, young or old, to work at even a part-time job for $5.50 or $6.00 an hour?

An increase in the mandated minimum wage to $6.15 per hour would be unprecedented in size: in effect, it would represent an increase of $1.90 per hour (44.7 percent) from 1996 to 1999. Never before has Congress raised the minimum wage by more than $1.05 per hour over a period of four years. And that $1.05-per-hour hike took place from 1978 to 1981, a period in which inflation was increasing an average of 10.7 percent per year.

Supporters of a federally mandated minimum wage continue to claim that additional increases are needed because the "rich are getting richer, while the poor are getting poorer." Although wage differences have widened over the past 20 years, such bad economic policy as a mandated minimum wage for workers serves only to exacerbate this problem. President Clinton's proposal to raise the minimum wage, moreover, works against the efforts of Congress to address the problem of moving unskilled Americans from welfare to work. It is an uncompassionate mandate that gives some low-wage workers an increase in their earnings while depriving others of the opportunity to earn anything at all.

Proponents often point to the increase in employment after the most recent hikes in the minimum wage as proof that raising the minimum wage does not destroy jobs. This argument, however, is misleading and deceptive. The overwhelming majority of economists agree that focusing only on the minimum wage's effect on total employment hides significant negative effects within groups like teenagers (see Chart). Although the last increase in the minimum wage did not reduce employment, it did reduce employment growth. The number of jobs, particularly for teenagers, would have grown even faster than it did over the past two years without the 1996 and 1997 increases in the minimum wage.

To be sure, increasing the minimum wage would help some low-income workers, but it would harm many more Americans. Consider the following:

- Had Congress not raised in the minimum wage in 1996, there would have been 128,000 more entry-level job opportunities for teenagers than were created otherwise. After the October 1996 increase, the employment rate of teenagers declined by 0.14 percent. For black teenage males, the decline was even worse—1.0 percent.

- Recent economic research suggests that a higher minimum wage would decrease school enrollment and increase the proportion of idle teenagers—those neither in school nor employed.

- Raising the minimum wage to $6.15 would cost consumers and workers about $6.5 billion over the next two fiscal years as the higher cost of entry-level jobs is passed on through higher prices and lower real wages. Although the overall inflation rate has been very modest in recent years, inflation in the service sector—

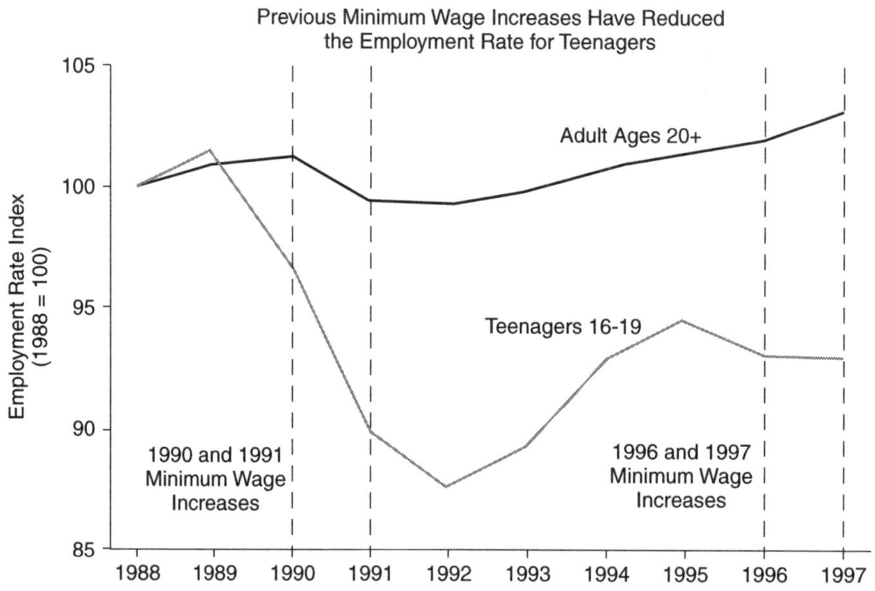

Note: In 1998, the employment rate for adults was 63.6% while the rate for teenagers was 46.8%.
Source: U.S. Department of Labor, Bureau of Labor Statistics.

in which most minimum wage workers are employed—is rising much faster.

- Increasing the minimum wage would represent a substantial unfunded mandate on state and local government. It would cost taxpayers about $383.1 million over the next two fiscal years as the higher cost of state and local government jobs is passed on through higher taxes or fewer services.

A policy decision like increasing the minimum wage is not cost-free someone has to pay for it. Economic research indicates that those who pay the most are unskilled youth through fewer job opportunities, consumers through higher prices, and taxpayers through higher taxes or fewer services. Voters recognize these costs. Over the past two years, they have rejected eight out of ten state and local ballot initiatives that would have raised the minimum wage. Instead of hiking the minimum wage, Congress and the Clinton Administration should take positive steps to benefit American workers. They should cut marginal tax rates on work, savings, and investment; increase the skills of the future workforce; modernize the Fair Labor Standards Act to grant working parents the opportunity for flexible work schedules; and reduce the burden of federal regulations.

Marginalism and the Morality of Pricing Human Lives

Dwight R. Lee

When I ask students in my large economics classes if some things are just too important to put a price on, someone always answers, "human life." This seems like a reasonable answer. After all, how many people would sacrifice their lives for cash, no matter how much was offered? What is the point of being a rich corpse? But economists reject the notion that human life is priceless. They put a price on human life, not because they are uncaring, callous, and completely lacking in moral sensitivity, but because they have a professional interest in understanding human action and because they understand that there is nothing morally lacking about pricing human life.

All of us put a price on our own lives every day with the choices we make and the actions we take. And pricing human life provides information that can save large numbers of lives, certainly not an immoral activity. Unfortunately, the moral superiority that so many people feel when expressing outrage at pricing human life helps keep in place government policies that cause many people to die needlessly.

Recognizing that prices reflect the marginal value of things is the key to understanding why economists put prices on human life. The price of asparagus gives us information on the value of one more pound of asparagus, not the value of the entire crop. Similarly, when economists talk about the price of human life, they are referring to the marginal value of life—the value of a slightly longer life expectancy—not the total value. The total value we put on our lives is extremely high (in most cases infinite), so we would not agree to be killed for any amount of money. Yet we put a very low marginal value on our lives. We routinely do things that reduce our life expectancy by marginal amounts in return for rather minor conveniences and pleasures. We often stay up too late, eat and drink too much, fail to get enough exercise, and drive too fast. When we do so, we are putting a price on our lives, and a pretty low price. Just how much is it worth to eat that extra cream puff or drink that extra beer? You would probably forgo the cream puff for $10, but not to avoid reducing your life expectancy by a marginal amount. If so, the implication is clear—the marginal value, or price, you place on your life is no more than $10.

The Risks of Government Policies to Reduce Risks

There is nothing wrong or irrational about putting a low marginal value on our lives. We face tradeoffs in everything we do, and living a meaningful and satisfying life requires doing things that reduce how long we can expect to live. It is sensible to avoid paying very much to avoid very small risks and the corresponding reductions in life expectancy.

In many situations we can choose how much to pay to avoid risks. We can choose to sacrifice time by slowing down a little, taking a somewhat less dangerous job that pays a little less, or buying a slip-resistant rubber mat for the bathtub (bathtubs are dangerous places). Government policy attempts to reduce many risks we face, but we have little choice in how much we pay for the risk reduction we receive. The justification for government action is that the risks are general, like the risks from pollution, and it would be difficult, if not impossible, for individuals to protect themselves acting alone. This is a reasonable justification for some risks, although it cannot be used for many government regulations, such as those requiring seat-belt use or outlawing smoking in all bars. But even when government action is justified, it doesn't make sense to enact regulations that make people pay more to reduce risks than the reduction is worth. Unfortunately, this is common practice.

According to many studies of how much people pay for safety devices and how much income they sacrifice to take safer jobs, they are willing to spend from $3 million to $7 million to save a life. Yet many government regulations impose a far greater cost per life saved. For example, Environmental Protection Agency (EPA) regulations on benzene storage are estimated to cost $260 million per life saved; EPA regulations on contaminated land disposal over $4.5 billion per life saved; and Occupational Safety and Health Administration (OSHA) regulations on formaldehyde over $92.7 billion per life saved! The problem with the high regulatory cost of saving a life is not only that these costs are far higher than the amount individuals would pay, but that these regulations increase the number of lives lost.

Such costly policies may reduce some risks, but they also reduce wealth, and there is plenty of evidence of a positive relationship between wealth and life expectancy. Obviously healthy people are more productive and therefore wealthier. But cause and effect also goes the other way; studies show that costly policies, by reducing our wealth, also reduce life expectancy, with an estimated one life lost for every $10 million to $50 million in regulation costs. Using the $50 million estimate, this implies that saving one life with the formaldehyde regulation would cause the loss of over 1,854 lives due to reduced wealth.

Another problem with extremely costly regulations to reduce risk brings us back to the importance of marginal considerations. When the marginal cost of saving life is higher with one regulation than with another, it is possible to save more lives at the same cost by reducing the high-marginal-cost regulation and expanding the low-marginal-cost regulation. For example, if the EPA land-disposal regulation (which saves fewer than three lies) were scrapped, and just a small portion of the $4.5 billion in saving were used to expand low-marginal-cost-per-life-saved regulation, thousands of additional lives could be saved and there would be a net reduction in government regulation. In addition, by reducing costly regulations, more resources would be available for the creation of wealth and this would save even more lives.

By refusing to put a price on human life government regulators can justify regulations with extremely high costs for a life saved. Despite the superficial morality suggested by this "save-a-life-at-any-cost" approach to regulation, the result is more lives lost than if the marginal cost of saving lives were considered—if a price were put on human life—when we legislate and implement regulations.

Kathie Lee's Children

William Anderson

Media personality Kathie Lee Gifford took quite a pounding when the National Labor Committee, a labor union organization, found that some of the clothes sold under her label in the U.S. were made by children in a Honduran "sweat shop."

Union lobbyists and their paid-for politicians paraded 15-year-old Wendy Diaz around Washington to testify about how badly the factory had treated her: long hours, few bathroom breaks, and 31 cents an hour. The unions then insisted that no more clothing be imported from this factory, or any similar one.

Gifford, now properly contrite, has devoted her life to ending child labor. She backs the UN's International Labor Organization bid for U.S. subsidies to enforce a global ban on employing young people, and otherwise implement its socialist charter. Gifford also promises to donate the profits from her clothing line, now made only by adults, to a myriad of liberal causes.

A few days after the Gifford story broke, the unions took advantage of the attention and stepped up their campaign. They said that basketball shoes bearing the name of Michael Jordan were made by overseas children making even less than Kathie Lee's kids.

But the story did not take off. The reason: Nike fought back. It pointed out that the workers in Pakistan who make Nike products earn five times the pay of other workers in that country. Far from exploiting children, Nike is actually doing the workers of Pakistan a great service.

Basic economic logic explains why. If young people and their families in the third world would be better off idle, they would stop working. If they could get higher wages for the same work, they would change jobs. If they could make a better investment in their future in some other way, they would do so. As it stands, however, these supposed "sweat shops" are the best thing that's happened to the third world in decades.

Let's return to the Gifford case. Ten years ago, Honduras had virtually no assembly plants. But with a booming international market for clothing, factories have sprung up all over the country to offer a way out of poverty and disease. Today, the country has 160 assembly plants that employ some 75,000 people.

Those lucky enough to work in these factories are doing well in a country where per capita income is $600 a year and unemployment is 40 percent. Plants routinely subsidize lunch, offer free medical care to employees, and are air conditioned—benefits unheard of in other lines of employment.

As one worker told the *New York Times*, "This has been an enormous advance for me, and I give thanks to the *maquila* [factory] for it. My monthly income is seven times what I made in the countryside, and I've gained 30 pounds since I started working here."

The labor force is extremely fluid, bid from factory to factory at ever higher wages. If a worker doesn't like the terms, he goes elsewhere. The owners try to make their working conditions better to attract the best employees. As factories invest more, and workers become more productive, they command a higher wage. Already, wages are on the rise in Honduras.

The denunciation of child labor assumes people in Honduras have the option of keeping their children fed and idle for 18 years. But this is fantasy. As Wendy Diaz herself said, she worked long hours to provide food and clothing for her two younger brothers, who might otherwise have starved.

Late in the day, she even urged the U.S. not to cut off trade, for fear the factories would have to shut down and her friends would be forced into prostitution. But the damage was already done: frightened by the U.S. media campaign, her former factory started laying off workers under 16 and stopped hiring altogether.

The issue of child labor is hardly new. In 1802, the British Parliament passed the first law against child labor in factories. It was the beginning of a legislative process that continues well into this century. Historians usually portray anti-child labor crusaders as humanitarians. On the contrary, they succeeded only in cutting off economic opportunity, and making children less valuable to their parents.

The pre-factory age was not a time of happy, contented kids. From 1730 to 1740, 75 percent of children in England died before age five. From 1810 to 1829, supposedly the evil age of the factory, infant mortality fell to 32 percent and would continue to drop. Capitalism and the industrial revolution gave youngsters a chance to survive.

Nassau Senior, one of the great British economists of the mid-1800s, noted that most of the agitation for the anti-child labor Factory Acts came from humanitarians, but from organizations of adults who wanted more textile work for themselves. "They got up therefore a frightful, and (as far as we have heard and seen) an utterly unfounded picture of the ill treatment of the children," Senior wrote.

So it is today. American labor unions and their allies paint a horrific picture, and they offer a theory of economics to back it up: by purchasing products made by exploited youngsters, American consumers are forcing them into a living Hell. Stop buying the products, make them in the U.S. instead, and the children will be free to play and go to school.

Factory owners in Bangladesh once faced international sanctions unless they stopped using child labor. Oxfam, the British charity, reported that the factories laid off 30,000 child workers. The children then took more dangerous jobs, with thousands becoming prostitutes or starving.

Like their English counterparts of 150 years ago, the unions who pinned Ms. Gifford to the wall have a dark, hidden agenda. Their goal is not to help children; it is to cut off imports, rip off American consumers, and pad their own wages at everyone else's expense. They have no plans for dealing with the problems of Honduras's children after they've been sent packing. As a union official shrugged to the *New York Times,* "I'm not an economist."

Ironically, when we hear accusations of child labor in Honduras, Pakistan, and Bangladesh, it's a sign that these countries are on the right track. It suggests they are becoming competitive with monopolistic unions here. But instead of competing fair and square, the unions turn to protectionist politics and media propaganda.

The best way to improve the lot of third-world children is not to boycott, but to buy the products of their labors. It is the old Kathie Lee Gifford, not the new and improved one, who is the real humanitarian.

Markets and Freedom

Dwight R. Lee

Economic Notions

The social cooperation that emerges in free markets permits the specialization on which prosperity depends. We would be much poorer without the specialization that is possible only when large numbers of people can coordinate production and consumption through market exchange. But even more important than the material wealth we realize from the marketplace is the benefit of freedom. We would soon be deprived of most of our freedom without the accountability and discipline possible only in market economies.

Freedom is easy to take for granted, especially in the United States where we have enjoyed what people in many other countries can only dream about. Freedom is a lot like good health: people tend not to appreciate it until they lose it. Just as healthy people can destroy their health by yielding to short-run temptations, free people can destroy their freedom by opting for short-run political advantages that undermine the conditions on which freedom depends.

Also, as important as wealth is, it is secondary to both good health and freedom. Wealth is of limited value to those without the health or the freedom to enjoy it.

Furthermore, good health and freedom are important elements in the production of wealth, with freedom being absolutely essential. Sick people can be productive, but without freedom the productive cooperation of the marketplace is impossible.

So I shall discuss two separate but related points in this column. First, the productive cooperation of the marketplace depends on freedom, and second, freedom depends on the productive cooperation of the marketplace. Economist typically have the unpleasant task of pointing to the tradeoffs that are the inevitable consequence of scarcity. But with wealth and freedom, there is no tradeoff, they reinforce each other in market economics, with it generally impossible to have one without the other.[1] Attempts to increase wealth with political policies that reduce freedom invariably end up reducing both.

Markets Require Freedom

Markets work their magic by allowing people to communicate the benefits they realize from the efforts of others and the costs of their efforts to benefit others. Ultimately, all benefits and costs are subjective, depending on people's preferences and circumstances which only they can accurately evaluate. This is obvious in the case of benefits. Who but the person who consumes a good, or avails himself of a service, is in a better position to judge the value of the benefits realized? But if benefits are subjective, then so are costs, which are nothing more than the value of forgone benefits. And since they are subjective, people can accurately communicate costs and benefits to one another only by having the freedom to enter into, or exit, different markets as they see fit, and to buy and sell at any mutually agreeable price. Government price controls restrict our freedoms as both buyers and sellers, and destroy wealth by censoring our communication with one another.

Central planning fails because people don't have the freedom to act on the local information that only they possess. When the central direction of political

[1]I have qualified this statement to account for the situation where a country possesses great wealth because of natural resource endowments and has an a autocratic political regime, suppressing the freedoms of its subjects. But even in this case, a the lack of freedom prevents the country from realizing the full benefit from its resources, and undermine the productivity necessary to expand, or even maintain, its wealth.

authorities is substituted for the market choices of individual producers and consumers, economic decisions are necessarily made in an informational vacuum. A productive economy requires the use of information that is dispersed throughout the population, and that information cannot be used without individual freedom. Destroy freedom and you destroy the information flows that are the essence of market economies.

Freedom Requries Markets

The connection between freedom and markets also runs the other way. Just as the market depends on freedom, so freedom depends on the market. Certainly private property, which is fundamental to all market economies, protects individual freedom. If the state owns all of the auditoriums and printing presses, how much freedom do you have to speak out against government policy? If the state owns all the means of production, how much freedom do you have to launch your own business? Start eliminating private property, and undermining the market that depends on it, and you start eliminating freedom.

But the market also protects freedom by establishing the only setting in which it can be tolerated. Freedom without responsibility is mere license, indulgence, and privilege, and will not long be tolerated. Real freedom, and the only freedom that can survive, is exercised in ways accountable to the concerns of all. The only freedom that satisfies this requirement is that which is subject to the discipline of the marketplace. Eliminate markets, and you eliminate the accountability necessary for freedom to survive.

For example, pollution problems result directly from not having markets in the use of the environment as a dump. If such markets existed, polluters would have to pay prices that reflected the cost their emissions imposed on others. Polluters would be accountable to others, and we could tolerate the freedom to discharge waste products into the environment. But because we don't have pollution markets, we accept government restrictions on polluting activities that would be unacceptable in most areas of our lives.

Our Freedoms Are Vulnerable

Freedoms are seldom taken away all at once. They are typically lost a little at a time, with people seldom noticing the loss. Even when freedom is reduced directly, as when government imposes occupational licensing in the name of protecting consumers, few people notice, and even if they do, they don't see the restrictions as affecting them. But as the great Austrian economist F. A. Hayek pointed out, "The benefits I derive from freedom are . . . largely the result of the uses of freedom by others."[2] For example, those who suffer the most when people lose their freedom to become barbers without having to pass state exams on the chemical composition of hair are not aspiring barbers, but people who need haircuts.

Also, there is an insidious dynamic to the loss of freedom. Direct restrictions always reduce freedom by more than is apparent because every restriction imperceptibly undermines the accountability of the marketplace that makes freedom possible.

Thomas Jefferson was correct when he said, "Eternal vigilance is the price of liberty." People are more likely to exercise vigilance in protection of their freedom when they understand the inextricable connection between it and the market.

[2]See F. A. Hayek, *The Constitution of Liberty* (Chicago: University of Chicago Press, 1960), p. 32.

Socialized Medicine Is the Problem

Walter Block

Recently, Canadian Prime Minister Jean Chrétien changed his mind about his country's system of socialized medicine. After long and hard opposition, he now favors a two-tier health system, including user fees and private provision. This makes it all the more important to take another look, not just at the surface of state-run medical care, but at its basic principles.

Ever since Vancouver Canuck hockey player Daniel Sedin jumped the health-care queue with his herniated and ruptured lower back disc, there has been an outbreak of wailing and gnashing of teeth on the part of defenders of socialized medicine. Nor was this the only such high-profile case. About a year ago Grizzlies basketball center Bryant "Big Country" Reeves hurt his ankle and was similarly catapulted to the head of the medical waiting list. But beyond such headline-grabbing cases there are numerous other privileged characters; politicians and bureaucrats and their families and friends with political pull and doctors, nurses, other health-care professionals, and those who can reply on them for favors. This is called "professional courtesy."

Most complaints have focused on the unfairness of a system that allows the privileged to receive medical care within a few days of an injury, while forcing others to wait weeks and even months, if not years. But this is exactly backward. The problem is not that some few people are treated quickly, as they should be. It's that we aren't all dealt with like members of an advanced civilization, where quick service is always the order of the day. We *all* should be treated like paying customers—and if we were, we would be.

Why are there long waiting lines that do not dissipate quickly? In economic parlance, this comes about because demand is greatly in excess of supply. There is no other reason; that is it: supply's falling short of demand is a necessary and sufficient cause of long and enduring queues.

But to answer in this manner is only to put off the inevitable question: why does demand continue to exceed supply in some markets but not in others? Again, the answer comes straight out of Economics 101: a permanent shortage arises and endures if and only if prices are pegged at below-equilibrium levels and kept there through force of law.

Some people think there is something special about medical care. There is not. Yes, if we do not avail ourselves of it, we will be in dire straits. But no less can be said for food, clothing, shelter, energy, transportation—you name it. And economic law, just as in the case of chemistry or physics, is no respecter of how important an industry is to human well-being; it works just the same in medical services as for paper clips or rubber bands. Impose artificially lower prices in a market—let alone virtually zero prices as in medicine—and you guarantee a shortage.

If any evidence of this phenomenon were needed, it has recently been furnished in three completely separate markets. Rent control pegs rents below market levels; it reduces incentives to supply additional residential rental units and decreases benefits to tenants who economize on space. The energy shortage in California stems entirely from the fact that retail prices are fixed at artificially low levels, thus retarding incentives on the part of customers to decrease their usage, and on the part of potential suppliers to bring more energy to this market.

Last but not least, and most relevant to our present concerns, is the health-care market in Canada. Here, too, consumers are prevented by law from paying prices that reflect the scarcity value of medical services. We do this, of course, out of misguided compassion. But this policy is based on blatant economic illiteracy. Canadians think they can violate economic law with impunity. They cannot.

Our much-vaunted (in coercive socialistic circles, that is) health-care system is predicated on a violation of economic principles. It is built on a foundation of quicksand.

Rescind Socialized Medicine

The only way to enable all citizens to enjoy the benefits now accorded only to a Sedin, a Reeves, or other medically privileged characters, is to completely rescind socialized medicine. It should be privatized and take its place among all other industries (cars, computers, chalk) that contribute mightily to our advanced standard of living, with no queues for anyone, thank you. This step would, with one fell swoop, radically reduce waiting lists and the brain-drain of Canadian doctors and nurses as well. Chrétien's recent conversion is too little too late if we want the health-care system to function as well as these other industries do.

Adam Smith's invisible hand of the market works its magic in every industry known to man. Health care is no exception. Those who take the opposite point of view are responsible for the needless suffering of the sick who cannot get timely help, thanks to medical socialism. This system did not work in the USSR. It cannot function with regard to Canadian health care either. Must we suffer through this for 70 years as the unfortunate Russians did? You don't like queue jumpers? Get used to it. It was part and parcel of the old Soviet system, and there is no way we can escape this if we copy the Soviets in health care.

At this point the critic will retort, "It is not fair to charge people market prices for health care; the rich will be treated better." But that is precisely the point of being rich in the first place. If the wealthy did not get better treatment, what would be the point in trying to amass riches? (And if they didn't try to amass riches, the entire economy would tank, not just health care.) In any case, the better off are already advantaged under the present system: they can jump queues in Canada or take their business to the United States.

Another objection: there's nothing for the poor in returning health care to the private sector. Nonsense. The poverty stricken are treated far better in capitalist countries than anywhere else, and medical service is again no exception. Yes, of course, the impecunious have to wait for the well-off to purchase MRIs (many small states in America have more of them than all of Canada does), but when they do, low-income people too can avail themselves of high-tech diagnostics. This is precisely why the poor have color televisions, computers, cars, and more. Had these too, been socialized, they would still be toys reserved for the rich.

The Problem with Price Controls

Bruce Bartlett

I remember hearing a speech back in 1980 by former Treasury Secretary John Connally, who was then running for president. At the time, inflation was running at double digits and there were widespread calls for price controls to deal with it. Connally denounced this effort in the strongest possible terms, saying price controls never work and only make the problem worse.

Well, like the kid who said the emperor wasn't wearing any clothes, I had to ask the former Treasury secretary why it was that he imposed price controls on the U.S. economy in 1971? It has been widely reported that among Richard Nixon's advisers, Connally was the strongest advocate of controls. He basically replied that while controls never work, there was this unique set of circumstances in August 1971, that never existed before and probably will never exist again, in which they could have worked.

I would have had a lot more respect for the guy if he had simply admitted that he was wrong. That is certainly the consensus view among economists. They believe that underlying inflationary forces can never be arrested through controls. All that happens is that prices catch-up after controls are ended, so that prices more or less end up in the same place eventually.

So widely accepted is this phenomenon that even the ultra-liberal *New York Times* accepts it. In an editorial on December 29, 1997, it denounced plans for price controls on cable rates, saying, "When controls are lifted—as eventually they must be—prices promptly make up for all lost ground." This was clearly the case with Nixon's controls.

Inflation fell from the 6 percent range before controls were imposed to the 3 percent range while controls were in place.

But by 1973, as controls broke down, inflation accelerated, hitting more than 12 percent in 1974 (see figure).

Controls break down in part because there are so many exceptions that must be made for the economy to function. Controls cannot be imposed on imports, for example, since foreigners are not subject to U.S. laws. This means that prices for critical materials, such as oil, can still rise despite controls, and that products using oil must also be allowed to rise. Exports must also be free of controls, lest foreigners simply buy up U.S. goods at controlled prices and resell them for market prices.

It makes no difference how diligently price controls are administered, they still break down. This has been the case throughout history, even when the death penalty applied to violations of them. A famous example survives from ancient Rome, when the Emperor Diocletian tried to do exactly that. And lest one believe that such extremism lies only in the distant past, in recent years both Iraq and Libya have imposed the death penalty for violating price controls.

Despite all this experience, the siren song of price controls still beckons the naive and self-serving. Even the Bush Administration, which initially opposed controls on electricity prices in California, succumbed to political pressure and imposed them there. But even though the price caps are just a few weeks old, they are already breaking down.

One problem is that they encourage excessive energy use. If people can buy any commodity for less than the market price, then by definition they are going to use more of it. This problem is exacerbated by California's blackout policy to deal with temporary energy shortages. At least 10,000 businesses have requested exemptions from these blackouts,

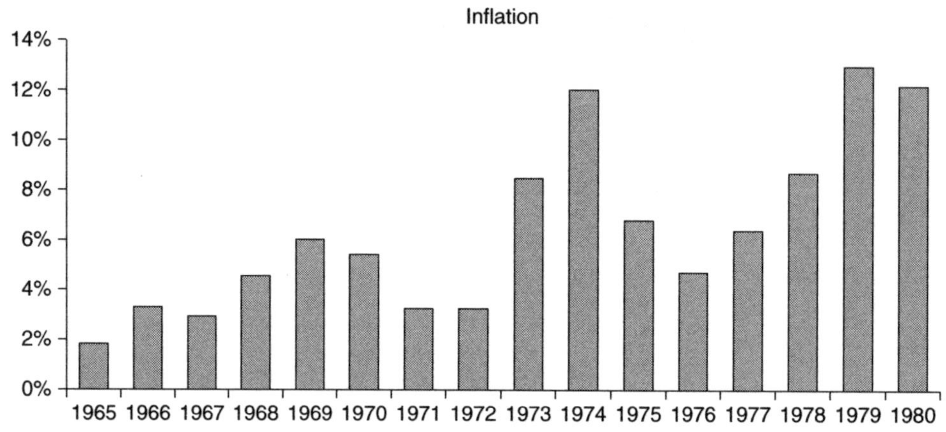

Source: Bureau of Labor Statistics.

which means that they will have to be more severe on those that have to comply with them. Also, some businesses are encouraged to waste energy, so that when the state forces them to cut back on energy use, they will have power to spare.

The longer price caps remain in place, their problems will only increase. They will reduce the incentive to produce more energy and inevitably lead to litigation, as lawyers argue about whether controls were properly complied with. These effects will last long after controls are lifted. California will forever be viewed as a riskier place to invest in power plants, meaning producers will have to get higher prices permanently to protect them against the risk of new controls. And the litigation may go on forever, too. It wasn't until 1995 that Occidental Petroleum settled a case involving its alleged violation of federal oil price controls in 1979.

In return for a bit of temporary relief, California and the federal government have embarked down a slippery slope. These temporary controls are likely to last much longer than anyone imagines, because the threat of catch-up price increases will be politically intolerable. But the longer controls last, the more severe their impact on energy supply.

Demand and Supply

Dwight R. Lee

Economic Notions

No series on the basic notions of economics can continue long without introducing demand and supply. These concepts, as illustrated with demand and supply curves, are fundamental to how economists understand economic behavior. In particular, with the use of demand and supply curves, I can supplement in concise and powerful ways my previous discussion of the communication, cooperation, and coordination of the marketplace.

The Basics of Demand and Supply

Although a complete discussion of demand and supply curves has to consider a number of complexities and qualifications, the essential notions behind these curves are straightforward. The demand curve is based on the observation that the lower the price of a product, the more of it people will demand. There may be occasional exceptions to this behavior (and indeed economists have developed the theoretical possibility of such and exception), but they are so few and transients that economists refer to the negative relationship between price and quantity demanded as the "law of demand." Because of the law of demand, demand curves (such as D in the figure) are always shown as downward sloping, with the price on the vertical axis and the quantity demanded (over some period) on the horizontal axis.

The basic notion behind the supply curve is that the higher the price of a product, the more of it producers will supply. In other words, as with the curve S in the figure, supply curves are upward sloping. A justification for this upward sloping relationship between price and quantity supplied is that the cost of producing additional units of the product increases as more is produced. So it takes a higher

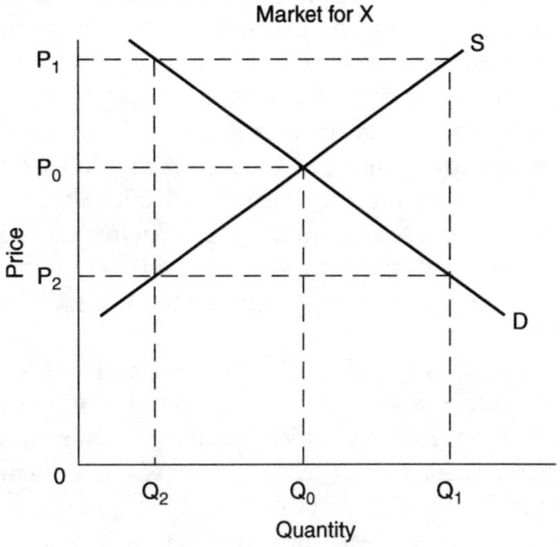

price to motivate additional output. But this is not necessarily the case when there is time for new firms to enter an industry, or for existing firms to expand their plant size. Such longrun adjustments to a higher price can permit more of the product to be made available at the original cost (or even a lower cost), in which case the supply is horizontal (or negatively sloped). But over periods of time that can extend to several months or more, it is reasonable to assume that supply curves slope upward.

Obviously, a lot of things affect the amount of a product that will be demanded and supplied besides its price. But for any set of demand and supply curves, all of these other influences are held constant, since the purpose of the analysis is to allow us to concentrate on the effects of the product's price on the amount demanded and supplied.

Communicating Through the Market

The simple diagram here allows us to consider the most important insight from demand and supply analysis, which is how people coordinate their decisions by communicating through market prices.

Assume that we start off with a price for denim jeans given by P_2, in the figure. The most important thing about that price from an economist's perspective is that it fails to coordinate the decisions of suppliers and consumers. At price P_2, suppliers are willing to supply only Q_2 pairs of jeans, but consumers want to buy Q_1 pairs. Consumers will be frustrated because they are unable to obtain all the jeans they want at the prevailing price, and in response to this frustration they will start bidding up the price of jeans relative to the price of other products. By doing so, they communicate to suppliers that they want more resources devoted to the production of additional jeans because they are worth more than what those resources are currently producing elsewhere. Suppliers respond appropriately to this information by moving up the supply curve, increasing the availability of jeans.

But the increase in price does more than communicate information from consumers to suppliers. It also is the means by which consumers communicate valuable information to one another. As consumers bid up the price of denim jeans, they are telling each other that these jeans are in short supply and that everyone should economize on their use, take better care of the ones they have, use substitute clothing, and so on. And consumers respond appropriately to this information by backing up the demand curve as they reduce the number of jeans they demand. This process continues to increase the price of denim jeans until it reaches P_0 in the figure, the price determined by the intersection of the demand and supply curves. This price is often called the equilibrium price, because at P_0 there is no pressure for the price either to increase or decrease. (Our discussion could have started at a price greater than P_0 and the communication would have taken the form of price decreases.) At P_0 we can clearly observe the miracle of market communication and cooperation. Millions of people pursuing their private advantages as consumers and producers, with almost no direct knowledge of, or interest in, the concerns and circumstances of others, are led to a completely coordinated pattern of decisions by responding to the information contained in market prices. Each consumer decides to consume an amount perfectly compatible with the amounts that all other consumers are deciding to consume and all producers are deciding to supply.

It's the Process

The equilibrium price, along with the equilibrium quantity Q_0 in the figure, is typically presented as the most important feature of demand and supply analysis. But seldom do real-world markets ever get to equilibrium. The world is constantly changing, and demand and supply curves constantly shift. Equilibrium is a moving target. The most important insight from demand and supply analysis is that the market process is constantly directing people to accommodate one another in ways that move them toward the coordination represented by equilibrium, and not just for one product, such as denim jeans, but for thousands of products. Things may not stay still long enough for equilibrium to be reached in any market. But freedom and market communication accomplish a pattern of cooperation that can never be duplicated by the coercion of central planning.

One of the best ways to appreciate the coordination and cooperation of market communication is by considering the problems that arise when political authorities censor it with price controls. In my next three columns, I'll use the demand-and-supply framework to examine those problems in detail.

PART

V

Economic Articles

Part V

- How to Reduce Unemployment, If We Want
- Inflation: One Man's Survey
- Government and High Prices
- A Message to Redistributionists
- The Truth About Tax Rates and the Politics of Class Warfare
- Capitalism and Culture
- The Nature of the Welfare State
- An Environment Without Property Rights

How to Reduce Unemployment, If We Want

Morgan Rose

Earlier this month, the U.S. Department of Labor released its latest unemployment report, which showed that across the country there were almost 200,000 fewer jobs in mid-September than there were in mid-August.[1] Very few of the household surveys used to calculate that figure were conducted after the September 11 terrorist attacks on the World Trade Center and the Pentagon, so job losses occurring as a direct or indirect result of those events will appear in upcoming months' reports. With some forecasts predicting that the unemployment rate will climb from today's 4.9% to 6% and above in the first half of next year,[2] it's worthwhile to use this space to make note of two sure-fire things we could do to lower the unemployment rate *if we want*.

That italicized phrase represents the main lesson to be made here, namely that economics is fundamentally about trade-offs between different things people want. An individual, community, or nation can almost always get more of something, but only at the cost of something else. We can raise the speed limits on our highways, but we have to be ready to accept more car accidents. For $20, you may be able to pay for three extra layers of cheese on your pizza, but only if you forgo the side order of buffalo wings. Reasonable people can come down on different sides of any given fence, but making a smart, informed decision on any issue means first recognizing what the relevant trade-offs are.

Concerning unemployment, minimum wage laws and unemployment benefits programs are two policies that are designed to benefit workers and those who want to work, respectively. The trade-off here is that both of these policies cause unemployment rates to be higher than they would be otherwise. It's a defensible position to argue that workers should be able to make enough money upon which to survive, or that public money should be used to lend a hand to people who find themselves between jobs. What advocates of those policies should be aware of, and what, as we will see below, economists have known for generations, is that embracing those policies implies embracing some additional people being without jobs.

The Trade-off Inherent to a Minimum Wage

A minimum wage makes employers less likely to hire someone by setting a lower limit on the amount that employers can pay employees. Some workers will be made better off with a higher wage, but workers whose labor is not considered to be worth as much as the law says they must be paid will find themselves without a job. A straightforward expression of this simple trade-off, written a quarter of a century before the Fair Labor Standards Act of 1938 established the first federally mandated minimum wage in the United States, is found in *Part IV, Chapter 21, paragraph 35* of *The Theory of Money and Credit* (1980, first pub. 1912) by Ludwig von Mises:

> If a man cannot sell his labor at the price he would like to get for it, he must lower the price he is asking for it or else he remains unemployed. If the government or labor unions fix wage rates at a higher point than the potential rate of the unhampered labor market and if they enforce their minimum-price decree by compulsion and coercion, a part of those who want to find jobs remain unemployed.

According to Mises, the only effective way to raise real wages is raising the amount of capital per worker used, something which occurs most

From www.econlib.org by Morgan J. Rose. Reprinted by permission of Morgan J. Rose.

effectively through the private choices of businesses and investors rather than through the intervention of government or labor unions.

Other authors, once establishing the trade-off between jobs and a minimum wage, go on to make explicit those they perceive as the winners or the losers of such a policy. In *Book III, Chapter 2, paragraph 48* of *The Common Sense of Political Economy* (1910), British economist Philip Wicksteed pointed a suspicious finger at "powerful Trade Unions" who had an interest in giving those with jobs a higher wage at the expense of those looking for jobs, while James Buchanan and Richard Wagner, in *Chapter 6, paragraph 65* of *Democracy in Deficit* (1977), remarked that "teenaged minority groups" would be most likely to benefit from a repeal of minimum wage laws.[3]

The Trade-off Inherent to Unemployment Benefits

Unemployment benefit plans, such as state-run unemployment programs in the United States, provide people who lose their jobs with income for some specified period of time, or until they find another job. Such benefit plans, also termed unemployment insurance, create a trade-off by encouraging some people to be out of work voluntarily. If you are insured against something bad happening to you, like being unemployed, then you will be less prone to prevent it from happening than you would be without the insurance. A person who knows he is eligible for unemployment benefits is more likely to leave his current job more readily, or once unemployed not search as actively for another job, preferring instead to live on the public's dime a while longer. Mises pointed out in *Part V, Chapter 34, paragraph 33* of *Socialism* (1981, first pub. 1922) that "in the case of unemployment insurance, the condition insured against can never develop unless the insured persons so will. If they . . . reduced their demands and changed their locations and occupations according to the requirements of the labour market, they could eventually find work." Unemployment benefits alter incentives such that people out of work may not face as much pressure to make the efforts and adjustments necessary to get another job as they would without the cushion provided by the government.

Frederic Bastiat took the idea of unemployment benefits altering incentives several steps further. In *Chapter 14, paragraphs 86–90* of *Economic Harmonies* (1996, first pub. 1851), he warned that the reliance on government, rather than on personal saving or private mutual-aid societies, for such funds would instill dependency on the part of workers. He feared that over time, workers "will become accustomed to considering unemployment benefits, not as something provided by the limited funds that they have accumulated by their own foresight, but as a debt that society owes them." Further, he worried that the government's need to deter people from taking advantage of a benefits program through fraud or laziness would lead inevitably to an expansion of government bureaucracy and intrusion into private lives.

Whether or not the implications of unemployment benefits are ultimately so dire, such a program definitely makes it cheaper for a person to choose unemployment over employment, and when the relative price of something falls, more people are attracted to it.

Finally, we have Alfred Marshall, who in *Book VI, Chapter XIII, paragraph 59* of his textbook *Principles of Economics* (1920) explicitly laid out the trade-off inherent under both a minimum wage and an unemployment benefit program:

> A scheme [for a minimum wage], that has any claim to be ready for practical adoption, must be based on statistical estimates of the numbers of those who under it would be forced to seek the aid of the State, because their work was not worth the minimum wage; with special reference to the question how many of these might have supported life fairly well if it had been possible to work with nature.

Summing Up

While several of the passages cited above reveal a pronounced opposition to minimum wage laws and unemployment benefits, they all make clear that there is an unambiguous trade-off between such government interventions and higher unemployment. An acknowledgment of that fact, that trade-offs exist and they matter regardless of your stance on particular positions, is a requirement for intelligent debate over unemployment or any other economic issue.

Notes

1. Steven Pearlstein, *Economists See Recession Now, and Worse Ahead,* Washington Post, 6 October 2001, p. E01.
2. Ibid.
3. For a recent study of the employment effects by age, race, and sex of the 1990–1991 minimum wage increase in the United States, see Donald Deere, Kevin M. Murphy, and Finis Welch, "Employment and the 1990–1991 Minimum Wage Hike," *American Economic Review,* Volume 85, No. 2, Papers and Proceedings of the Hundredth and Seventh Annual Meeting of the American Economic Association, Washington, D.C., January 6–8, 1995, (May, 1995), pp. 232–237. For a survey of theoretic and empirical studies of minimum wage laws, see Brown, Charles, Curtis Gilroy, and Andrew Kohen, "The Effect of the Minimum Wage Law on Employment and Unemployment," *Journal of Economic Literature,* June 1982, 20, pp. 487–528 (available online through *JSTOR* at many university libraries or by subscription).

Inflation: One Man's Survey

Ivan Pongracic

My Latin professor once taught me the golden rule of Roman emperors, *Julius cult decipi, ergo decipiatur.* It means the masses want to be cheated, so let's cheat them. Machiavelli built his theory of government partially on this credo.

Our modern emperors and Machiavellis use the same wisdom today. Why bother the masses with something they don't understand? If they did understand it, they would only be upset. So they spare us the truth, and it is pert enough to listen to Sunday talk shows to know how far they're willing to go in this effort.

The latest case is inflation.

According to our emperors, the "truth" is that inflation is under control. In fact, we might need to worry more about deflation, because the economy is even more productive than the government data show. "We are begging to reach a point," says former Fed governor Wayne Angell, "where the lack of inflation is baked into the system."

The Fed's low interest rate policy has produced optimism among investors who are presently enjoying the best of times. As the stock market goes up, people feel richer and more optimistic, so they buy more. The increased demand pushes up production and employment, and the stock market goes ever higher, increasing the good feeling and so on ad infinitum. If the Fed loosens the money supply even further, predicts Angell, "stock prices will go higher."

Well, as Lew Rockwell says, "academic fraud has never been more acceptable. "To prove that the government can create a permanent prosperity by creating money, our best and brightest economists are not just telling us that inflation is low, but that the government is even overstating it. To sound scientific (that is, precise), they tell us it is exactly 1.1 percent overstated. The government admits that inflation is running 3 percent. Keep in mind that these are people who don't have the slightest idea what is happening in real life.

Congress and the White House may have temporarily abandoned the attempt to fiddle with the data (for purposes of bringing in new revenue and lowering cost of living adjustments). But this issue is far from gone. We can expect it to be brought up at every subsequent budget negotiation.

Now, followers of Ludwig van Mises know that it is impossible to measure "inflation," even in the long run. To pretend to "measure" it from month to month is simply ridiculous. It is even more ridiculous when you consider how inflation is actually measured. Reading the *Wall Street Journal's* account of how "federal sleuths" find out the inflation rate, you have the feeling of reading the *Tirana Daily* (Albania being famous for its scientific approach to economics). "Government gumshoes" cover hundreds of miles monthly and visit hundreds of shops to find out changes in prices. Using "arm-twisting tricks," they "interrogate" shop-owners, landlords, salesmen, even chiropractic receptionists to reveal the true prices. Then, "each month some 90,000 prices are shipped to Washington, plugged into a computer, scrutinized, aggregated, adjusted for seasonal ups or downs, and then spit out as the monthly CPI report."

That's it: thousands of housewives and other part-timers collect some dubious numbers, federal government bureaucrats perform a statistical magic trick, and we get the CPI. Is it really possible that a country with literally billions of products and services, with most of their prices changing daily, would pretend to know average prices on a monthly basis? Well, *Julius vul, de-cipi, ergo decipiatur.*

So, I decided to perform a little experiment on my own, My method of "measuring" inflation could not, methodologically speaking, be much worse than the government's. Another reason for my suspicion

From *The Free Market*, May/June 1997, Vol. 15, No. 5. Reprinted by permission of Ludwig von Mises Institute.

was my car. In June of 1993 I bought a brand new Cavalier for $9,000 (excluding taxes). In June of 1996, the same dealer invited me to visit the premises and promised to change my oil for free. He wanted me to trade in my old Cavalier and buy a new one. I chose the same model of Cavalier, with the same amenities as in 1993, and took it for a spin. (Typically, he would not discuss the price before I tried it.) When I came back he hit me with the total—. In three years the price of my car had gone up 50 percent. And the government, and the economists, were telling me that the inflation rate is 3 percent a year. So I went to check some other prices, and found some other surprises. On January 20, 1993, a gallon of unleaded gasoline was 79 cents in Marion, Indiana; on January 20, 1997, it $1.29—more that a 50 percent increase.

Next I went to change my oil, and asked the shop owner to check the prices for the oil change in 1993. It was $7.95. This time he charged me $25—an increase of more than 220 percent.

I asked a financial officer at my university to give me the prices of tuition, board and room at our university. They rose from $11,648 to $14,402—an increase of approximately 25 percent.

And they have soared more than 250 percent since I started teaching in 1986. Government "admits" that tuition rose 141 percent from 1980 to 1990, or on an average annual rate of 8.6 percent, while the overall inflation was 3.1 percent.

During a visit to my dentist I asked him to give me the prices of some of his "basic" services. He agreed. The cleaning went from $55 to $70—an increase of 27 percent. Root canals went from $405 to $503—an increase of 24 percent. Composite white filling went from $114 to $149—a 30 percent increase. X-rays went from $48 to $61—a 33 percent increase.

I went back to the *Wall Street Journal* and compared the Markets Diary on January 20, 1993, and the Commodities Index was 202; on January 20, 1997, it was 242—an increase of close to 20 percent. Gold was $330 an ounce in 1993, and $354 in 1997. Gold was one of the main reasons for mainstream economists to declare inflation nonexistent.

Then I checked stock prices. The market went from 3241.95 to 6843.87—more than a 100 percent increase. The asset inflation, as Alan Greenspan himself is now realizing, can be as dangerous as any other inflation, and he is warning the investors about "irresponsible exuberance," only to be told, according to the *Wall Street Journal*, to "butt out."

So, the prices are rising, but the government doesn't want to bother us with the details. If you have to buy a car, have some kids in college, have bad teeth, travel a lot, and want to invest some money, your life could be some 40 percent more expensive than four years ago, but you can sleep in peace—inflation is under control—overstated even!

Still, "academic" economists sing nearly in unison: the CPI overstates the inflation by 1.1 percent. The *Wall Street Journal* did find one dissenting voice. The chief economist of Morgan Stanley Group, Stephen Roach, maintained that "the mother of all biases, housing, accounting for about 40 percent of the basket of measured goods and services, is vastly understated."

While government estimated that "the CPI's housing component rose by just 3 percent," Roach showed that "the average price of a newly built home rose by about 5 percent, the sharpest gain in seven years. And "prices for existing residences jumped by 6 percent, the largest gain in five years." So, according to Roach, "the CPI is not 3 percent but 3.4 percent or 3.6 percent."

But what if academic economists are wrong and inflation is much higher? First, the Fed would have to raise interest rates, since the real interest rates would presently be below zero. (The fact that cheap money is already wreaking havoc on the market is best seen by the number of bankruptcies. Bankruptcies are up nearly four-fold since 1984. More than one million Americans filed for personal bankruptcy in 1997.

Second, contrary to the New Era thinking of the mass media, the house of cards called the stock market will collapse. Banks will be stuck with bad loans, and another serious recession will threaten. Most importantly, the Clinton-Rubin-Greenspan economic miracle will be shown as another example of monetary cranks devising a method for making everybody prosperous by expanding credit. As Mises explained, people unfamiliar with economic law think that increasing the quantity of money in circulation can bring about permanent prosperity without the ill-effects of business cycles or rising prices. "This theory is utterly illusory," writes Mises. "But it guides the monetary and credit policy of almost every contemporary government."

Government and High Prices

Thomas J. DiLorenzo

The U.S. Congress is holding hearings on why gasoline prices have risen; pundits are beginning to repeat the anti-capitalist oil company bashing of the 1970s; and the U.S. Department of Housing and Urban Development (HUD) recently issued a report blaming prosperity for rising housing prices and self-servingly calling for more HUD subsidies for "the poor."

The Washington establishment has been quick to blame "greedy oil companies" and American prosperity for higher gas and housing prices, but the government itself is at fault with its policies of government-mandated price increases.

Urged on by American environmentalists' hate affair with the automobile, the U.S. government has employed every possible means to restrict the supply and drive up the price of gasoline. Regulation places over 90 percent of the outercontinental shelf off the California coast off limits to oil exploration; there are massive oil deposits in Alaska which are also off limits for exploration despite the fact that the existing oil wells there are being bled dry; and a myriad of other environmental regulations imposed on the oil industry drive up the costs of oil production.

For example, the government recently mandated that "reformulated" gasoline be sold in many areas of the U.S., which caused an immediate 10 cents per gallon price increase. American motorists have also been paying at least another 10 cents more per gallon of gas because of another Environmental Protection Agency (EPA) mandate for "oxygenated fuel," which the EPA itself claimed even before it issued the mandate contains Methyl Tertiary Butyl Ether, a water contaminant and potential health hazard. Gasoline taxes add as much as another 75 cents per gallon in some states.

Tax cuts and deregulation are the obvious means to deal with rising gasoline prices, but that would diminish the power and influence of the state, so it is not likely to be achieved.

Housing prices have gone up sharply in some American markets because of increased demand for housing fueled by rising prosperity. Normally, after a short lag, housing supply increases will follow, which would moderate the price increases. But zoning, building code, and environmental regulations have made it more difficult and costly to build houses. More ominously, there is currently a nationwide governmental movement to dramatically reduce the supply and increase the cost of housing under the rubric of "smart-growth" regulation, one of the dumbest ideas to be hatched by the state in many years.

Motivated in part by the environmentalist hatred of the automobile, so-called smart-growth proponents, which include dozens of governors, hundreds of local government officials, and Vice President Al Gore, want to force much of the population back into the cities (and presumably out of their automobiles and into mass transit) by using regulation to drive up the costs of housing in the suburbs.

Consequently, they have proposed or adopted extra real estate development taxes; urban "growth boundaries," beyond which development simply cannot take place; regulatory pressures on banks to get them to make fewer suburban and more urban real estate loans; revision of zoning laws to make suburban development more costly; state and federal land purchases which place more and more land off limits for residential use; prohibitions on the sale of farmland to developers; minimum-lot zoning regulation, including "superzoning" in such places as Marin County, California, where 60-acre lots are required in some parts of the county; utility hook-up "moratoria"; and endangered species lawsuits which stop development.

If such policies succeed in driving up suburban housing prices and causing a migration to the cities, housing prices will rise there, too, because of the increased demand and a supply that is even more restricted by regulation than in suburban housing markets.

Such policies were championed by the California state and local governments in the 1970s, with the result being a 500 percent increase in lot prices from 1972 to 1978. More recently, Portland, Oregon has become the "Mecca" of "smart-growth" regulation; lot prices there doubled from 1990 to 1995, and the increase in housing prices during that period was three times the rate of housing price increases of a decade earlier. Of the 50 largest metropolitan areas in the U.S., Portland experienced the fifth-highest rate of housing price appreciation from 1990 to 1995.

The politicians who are now acting indignant over rising housing and gasoline prices are, as usual, playing American citizens for suckers by offering even more intervention as the "solution." It is their own out-of-control regulations, coupled with the Fed's expansionist monetary policies, that are the real culprits. While persecuting companies like Microsoft for cutting prices, the government itself is the dominant cause of higher or "monopolistic" prices. Naturally, it exempts itself from antitrust prosecution.

A Message to Redistributionists

P. J. O'Rourke

Cato is about ideas. We spend a lot of time talking and thinking about ideas, but not just good ideas. Bad ideas are important, too. In fact, a lot of life operates on bad ideas. And I thought I'd like to talk about a bad idea: closing the global wealth gap. That is a very bad idea.

I mean, do we want to close the beauty gap and make everybody look like Dick Morris? Do we want to close the virtue gap and encourage Mother Teresa to have a deathbed affair, or appoint that Kennedy kid, Michael, to run the Save the Children Foundation? Do we want to close the talent gap and have an NBA full of players who have the height and talent of, for instance, me? If we had a world without gaps, where everyone was the same color, size, social class, and sex, who would get pregnant? If everyone had the same information, what would we talk about? Consider what would happen if everyone had the same work, the same job. Everyone would take the same vacation. You would have 5.8 billion people headed to the shore in the first two weeks of August, playing a game of beach volleyball—2.9 billion to a side. The idea of a world where all people are alike, which is essentially the idea that we fight against at Cato, is a fantasy for the stupid. But I'll tell you, egalitarianism is worse than stupid, it's immoral.

I think the Old Testament is quite clear about that. The Bible might seem to be a strange place to be doing economic research, but I have been thinking, from a political economy point of view, about the Tenth Commandment. Now the first nine commandments concern theological principles—thou shall not steal and kill and so forth. Fair enough. Then there's the Tenth Commandment: "Thou shall not covet they neighbor's wife. Thou shall not covet thy neighbor's house, nor his manservant, nor his maid-servant, nor his ox, nor his ass, nor anything that is thy neighbor's." I mean, here are God's basic rules for how we should live, a very brief list of sacred obligations and solemn moral precepts, and right at the end of it is: "Don't envy your buddy his cow." What is that doing there? Why would God, with just 10 things to tell Moses, choose jealousy about the stuff the guy next door has? Well, think about how important to the well-being of a community that commandment actually is. What that commandment says is that if you want a donkey, if you want a pot roast, if you want a cleaning lady, don't bitch about it, go get your own!

The Tenth Commandment sends a message to socialists to collectivists, to people who believe that wealth is best obtained by redistribution, and that message is clear and concise: Go to hell! It's as simple as that.

Egalitarianism is sinful; it's also cowardly. We fear the power that others have over us, and since wealth is power, the egalitarians fear the rich. They're afraid that Kathie Lee Gifford is going to make them sew jogging suits in sweat shops for 30 cents an hour. But, seriously, how rational is fear of the rich? Let's take a midnight stroll through a rich neighborhood. And let's take a midnight stroll through a poor neighborhood just a few blocks from here. Sure, you can get in a lot of trouble in Monte Carlo. You can lose at roulette or get suckered into a shady business deal with Princes Stephanie's husband. But you are a lot more likely to get mugged here in Northwest Washington. Now, mind you, I don't think we should begrudge the crimes of those poor people down the street. They're just practicing a little free-lance socialism; they're just being liberal Democrats in their own small way.

But the point is that the real alternative to the power of the rich is not power of the poor. It's just plain power. If we don't want the world's wealth to be controlled by people with money, then the alternative is to have the world's wealth controlled by people with guns. And governments have guns. They have quite a few guns. Now, in theory, it is fine that the government has guns and that the guns control money because, in theory, the mugger puts his pistol down and picks up a ballot and he steals from multinational corporations instead of from you. But the reality is obviously quite different. The track record of collectivist societies in the 20th century speaks entirely for itself. Thirty million dead from closing the wealth gap in Chinese agriculture; 6 million dead from closing the commerce gap in the Ukraine; and the deaths go on and on. Even the most democratic government becomes a law unto itself, and I don't think I really need to elaborate on that. At this moment Bill and Hillary are headed over to the Sidwell Friends School to hawk the Lincoln bedroom to Chelsea's friends. ("Okay, bring your pajamas, s'mores, and a hundred thousand dollars.")

Such are the products of envy and fear, which brings me to the third mainspring of egalitarianism: greed. And by greed I don't mean the simple lust for material objects. I am concerned about the greed for position and pride, for what nowadays is called self-esteem. I wonder how many of the people who profess to believe in the leveling ideas of collectivism and egalitarianism really just believe that they themselves are good for nothing. I mean, how many leftists are animated by a quite reasonable self-loathing? In their hearts they know that they are not going to become scholars or inventors or industrialists or even ordinary good kind people. So they need a way to achieve that smugness for which the left is so justifiably famous. They need a way to achieve self-esteem without merit. Well, there is politics. In an egalitarian world everything will be controlled by politics, and politics requires no merit.

Consider the four men who have been America's most prominent politicians in this past year: Bob Dole, Newt Gingrich, Al Gore, and Bill Clinton. Would you hire any of those men? Would you hire any of them to mow your lawn? Bob Dole would be down on his hands and knees trying to make a deal with the grass not to grow. Gore would be asking the cat if dandelions are an endangered species. Newt would borrow the Toro. And Clinton wouldn't be able to make up his mind. Power mower or push? Do the front first or the back? Rake and then mow, or the other way around? So he'd give up and he'd be in your kitchen raiding the refrigerator, flirting with your baby sitter.

We have to kill ideas like the wealth gap. The world doesn't need to be thinking about the wealth gap; the world needs to be thinking about wealth. Wealth is good. Everybody knows that about his own wealth. Wealth improves your life; it improves your family's life. You invest in wise and worthwhile things, and you help your friends and neighbors. Your life would get better if you got rich, and the lives of all the people around you would get better if you got rich. Your wealth is good. So why isn't everybody else's wealth good, too? I don't get it. Wealth is good when a lot of people have it, and wealth is good when just a few people have it. And that is because money is a tool, nothing more. I mean, you can't eat money, you can't sleep with it, you can't wear it as underwear very comfortably. And wealth, accumulation of money, is a bunch of tools. Now when one person, a carpenter for instance, has a bunch of tools, we don't say to him, "You have too many tools. You should give some of your saws and drills and chisels to the guy who is cooking the omelets." We don't try to close the tool gap.

Wealth has brought enormous benefits to the world. Rich people are heroes—especially if they donate some money to Cato. Those rich heroes didn't necessarily mean to be heroes, but that's beside the point. They are heroes, and yet the way we treat wealthy people in our political systems is terrible. Even now that the whole world has come to believe that free markets and private money making are good things, we still have our residual infatuation with equality and our proposals to close wealth gaps.

The Truth About Tax Rates and the Politics of Class Warfare

Daniel J. Mitchell, Ph.D.

President George W. Bush, holding firmly to his campaign commitment, has proposed a tax reform package that will strengthen America's economy. The across-the-board reductions in personal income tax rates he is seeking will increase incentives to work, save, and invest; and repealing the death tax will eliminate a pernicious form of double taxation while encouraging entrepreneurs and small-business owners to make decisions based on economic value instead of tax considerations.

These commonsense tax reforms are being criticized, however, by opponents of tax relief who claim that "only the rich" will benefit. Policymakers should ignore this class-warfare rhetoric. Unlike European welfare states crippled by redistributionist policies, the United States has prospered because success is admired rather than envied. But more needs to be done to redesign America's tax code so that barriers to upward mobility that remain are reduced. In other words, cutting taxes is not a policy for the rich, but a strategy that will help everyone else become rich or at least rise as far and as fast as their talent, ability, and willingness to work will take them.

The debate over tax "fairness" is not just an ethical battle between those who support a free-market economy and those who desire a welfare state. It is also an empirical battle based on numbers that often can be verified or disqualified. Not surprisingly, it turns out that many of the claims made by opponents of tax cuts do not withstand close scrutiny. For instance:

Myth: The rich do not pay their fair share of taxes and therefore should not get a significant share of a tax cut.

Reality: According to data from the Internal Revenue Service,[1] the top 1 percent of income earners pay nearly 35 percent of the income tax burden; the top 10 percent pay 65 percent; and the top 25 percent pay nearly 83 percent. The bottom 50 percent of income earners, on the other hand, pay barely 4 percent of income taxes. By definition, then, it is impossible to cut taxes without the so-called rich receiving a share of the benefits.

Myth: Lower tax rates will mean that the rich pay less.

Reality: This outcome depends on how much tax rates are reduced. History indicates that the revenue-maximizing rate is less than 30 percent.[2] In other words, when marginal rates are higher than 30 percent, the rich probably will pay more taxes if rates are lowered. The reason? There is less incentive to hide, shelter, or underreport income.

Consider what happened in the years following each of the three times Americans enjoyed significant tax rate reductions.

The 1920s: The top tax rate fell from 73 percent to 25 percent, yet the rich (in those days, individuals earning $50,000 or more) went from paying 44.2 percent of the tax burden in 1921 to paying more than 78 percent in 1928.[3]

The 1960s: After President John F. Kennedy slashed the top tax rate from 91 percent to 70 percent, those making more than $50,000 annually saw their tax payments rise during the next three years by 57 percent and their share of the tax burden climb from 11.6 percent to 15.1 percent.[4]

The 1980s: The top tax rate fell from 70 percent in 1980 to 28 percent in 1988 during the Reagan years. What happened to the "rich"? The top 1 percent went from shouldering 17.6 percent of the income tax burden in 1981 to paying 27.5 percent of the total in 1988. The top 10 percent saw their share of the burden climb from 48 percent in 1981 to 57.2 percent in 1988.[5]

Myth: Reducing income tax rates will not help the poor.

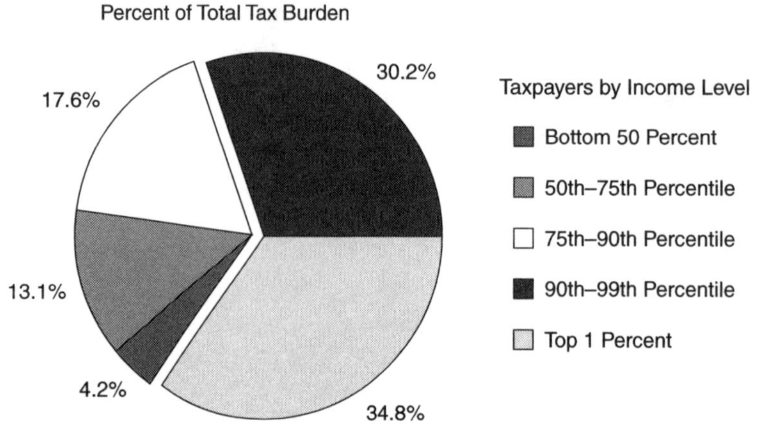

CHART 1 Top Ten Percent of Taxpayers Shoulder Nearly Two-Thirds of the Income Tax Burden
Source: The Tax Foundation, "Distribution of the Federal Individual Income Tax," Special Report No. 101, November 2000.

Reality: It is true that the poor will not receive a tax cut when tax rates are reduced, but the reason is that they do not pay income taxes. This does not mean, however, that they will receive no benefits from a tax cut. Indeed, because they are on the lowest rungs of the economic ladder, they will be the biggest beneficiaries of the faster growth that follows a tax cut.

Myth: The payroll tax is the biggest imposition on low-income workers, so reducing income taxes will have little effect on their tax burden.

Reality: This actually is true, but it is not an argument against reducing income tax rates. Instead, it is a reason to reform the Social Security system so that lower-income workers can build wealth and enjoy a more comfortable retirement.

Myth: Only millionaires are concerned about the tax-the-rich issue.

Reality: Like fairness, "rich" is a subjective term, but the most common definition of "rich" in Washington is someone in the top 20 percent (or quintile) of income. Many Americans in this quintile hardly would quality as rich, though, since the cutoff in 1999 for the top 20 percent of tax returns is $79,375 of household income. This quintile also includes many businesses—such as partnerships, sole proprietorships, and Subchapter S corporations—that use the personal income tax instead of the corporate income tax to file their returns. Most of these small-business owners do not satisfy the conventional definitions of wealthy, but most of them care greatly about tax reform and lowering tax rates. So do millions of middle-class families that are mischaracterized as rich by proponents of class welfare.

Myth: Lower tax rates mean the rich will get richer while the poor get poorer.

Reality: President Kennedy was right: A rising tide lifts all boats. Census Bureau data show that earnings for all income classes tend to rise and fall in unison.[6] In other words, economic policy either generates positive results, in which case all income classes benefit, or causes stagnation and decline, in which case all groups suffer. As Chart 3 illustrates, the high tax policies of the late 1970s and early 1980s are associated with weak economic performance, while the low tax rates of the 1980s are correlated with rising incomes for all quintiles. Likewise, all income groups enjoyed increases in income after the 1997 capital gains tax cut.

Myth: Lower tax rates will lead to a repeat of the failed policies of the 1980s.

Reality: In the 1980s, tax revenues climbed by 99.4 percent, much faster than was needed to keep pace with inflation. More important, the economy rebounded from the malaise of the 1970s. Indeed, the prosperity Americans enjoy today is a continuing legacy of th economic renaissance triggered by President Reagan's tax rate reductions.[7]

Myth: Eliminating capital gains taxes, death taxes, the double taxation of dividends, or the double taxation of savings will merely create loopholes for the rich to expolit.

Reality: Existing provisions of the tax code dealing with capital have the effect of taxing income more than once. More specifically, they impose multiple layers of taxation on savings and investment. Defenders of the status quo argue that these provisions are desirable. They can claim that the goal of income redistribution necessitates double taxation. They can even say that there is nothing morally wrong or economically destructive about discriminating against taxpayers who save and invest. They cannot argue legitimately, however, that elimination of double taxation creates loopholes. Double taxation is a bias; adopting policies that tax income only once will institute fairness in the code.

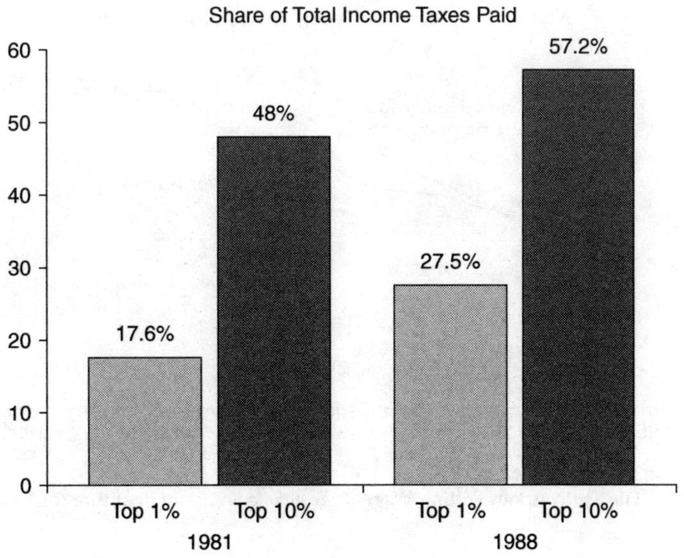

CHART 2 Rich Pay Greater Share of Income Tax Burden After Reagan Tax Cuts
Source: Internal Revenue Service.

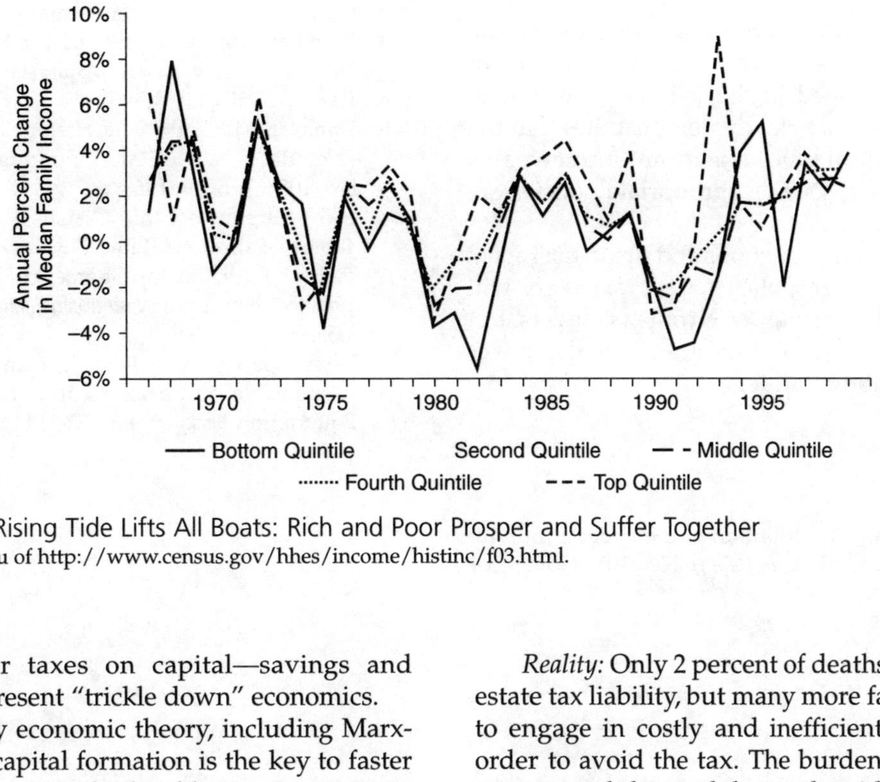

CHART 3 A Rising Tide Lifts All Boats: Rich and Poor Prosper and Suffer Together
Source: Census Bureau of http://www.census.gov/hhes/income/histinc/f03.html.

Myth: Lower taxes on capital—savings and investment—represent "trickle down" economics.

Reality: Every economic theory, including Marxism, agrees that capital formation is the key to faster growth and higher standards of living. Increases in real wages over time are closely correlated with the average amount of capital available per worker, (See Chart 4.) In other words, if workers are paid on the basis of what they produce, it makes sense to adopt tax policies that encourage investment in the tools, equipment, machinery, and technology that help them produce more.

Myth: The death tax effects only the very rich.

Reality: Only 2 percent of deaths may result in an estate tax liability, but many more families are forced to engage in costly and inefficient tax planning in order to avoid the tax. The burden of the tax, however, extends beyond those who either face the tax or take steps to avoid it. The death tax affects every family that lives in a community where a family-owned business must be liquidated to pay the tax. The death tax affects every worker when investments are sent offshore as families seek to protect their assets from this unfair form of double taxation. And the death tax affects everyone who loses income because a significant amount of money is invested

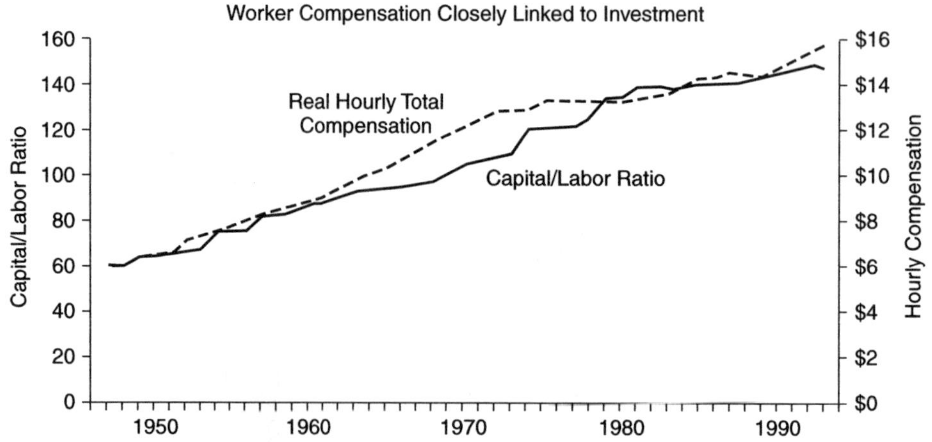

Note: Capital/Labor ration = Amount of capital per worker.
Source: Aldona and Gary Robbins. "The Truth About Falling Wages," *Economic Scorecard*, Institute for Policy Innovation, TaxAction Analysis, Third Quarter 1995.

for tax-minimization and tax-avoidance purposes instead of wealth-creation purposes.

Conclusion

When politicians pit one group against another, the only winners are those who believe that more power should be concentrated in the federal government. The economic evidence clearly demonstrates that the U.S. economy will produce significant income gains for all Americans as long as appropriate policies are followed.

Marginal tax rate reductions and death tax repeal are examples of those policies. Yes, taxpayers will benefit, including some upper-income taxpayers, but the real winners will be Americans on the lower rungs of the economic ladder.

Notes

1. Tax Foundation, "Distribution of the Federal Individual Income Tax," *Special Report* No. 101, November 2000.
2. The goal of legislators should not be to set the rate at the revenue-maximizing level; instead, they should lower rates even further to maximize growth. Regardless of the goal, however, it is self-defeating to set the top rate above the revenue-maximizing level.
3. Joint Economic Committee, "The Mellon and Kennedy Tax Cuts: A Review and Analysis," June 18, 1962.
4. *Ibid.*
5. Daniel J. Mitchell, "The Historical Lessons of Lower Tax Rates," Heritage Foundation *Backgrounder* No. 1086, July 19, 1966, p. 7.
6. U.S. Bureau of the Census, "Historical income Tables—Families." Table F-3, Mean Income Received by Each Fifth and Top 5 Percent of Families (All Races): 1966 to 1999, at *http://www.census.ov/hhes/income/histinc/f03.html.*
7. Peter Sperry, "The Real Reagan Economic Record: Responsible and Successful Fiscal Policy," Heritage Foundation *Backgrounder* No. 1414, March 1, 2001.

Capitalism and Culture

Llewellyn H. Rockwell, Jr.

From Left and Right, capitalism is condemned for all the cultural failings of the modern world—everything from mindless TV to dirty books to slatternly art to trashy movies to debasing music. It's an extension of the liberal habit of blaming a system for what are actually the failings of individuals.

Ludwig von Mises identified Victorian art critic John Ruskin as the intellectual source of this ceaseless griping. Ruskin saw civilization, embodied in the arts, as going down the tubes, and he labeled the market economy as the cause. This allowed him to be a socialist without surrendering upper-class affectations or having to prattle about workers and peasants.

Ruskin thus qualifies, said Mises, as "one of the gravediggers of British freedom, civilization and prosperity." "A wretched character in his private no less than in his public life," Ruskin eulogized the ancient producer cartels called guilds. "Government and cooperation are in all things the laws of life," wrote Ruskin in *Unto This Last* (1862), "anarchy and competition the laws of death."

Nowadays, practically everyone with a college degree is a tacit Ruskinian. Americans may understand the productive power of the market, but many are blind to its virtue as a civilizing agent, to its ability to sustain tradition, create what's beautiful and grand, and preserve what's right and good.

The Left (still essentially Marxian) wants us to think of capitalism as modern and industrial. More correctly, capitalism is just a name for the social recognition of private property, trade, and contract enforcement. It was as much a part of ancient Athens as 19th-century America. In its total absence, civilization would crumble, and the arts vanish.

In modern times, the confusion usually starts this way. Someone flips on the television to find the usual rotten show and offensive commercials. He concludes that's the market at work base, vulgar, and insulting to our intelligence.

Once on this trade, the anticapitalist mentality runs wild. The decadence of the cash nexus appears everywhere. Strip malls and yellow M's in the sky. Boxing, mashing, tabloids, rap, and low pay for intellectuals. It's all horrible, sniffs this person, and it's all capitalism's fault.

If this theory were correct, the prophets, saints, and ancient philosophers were wasting their breath. They called on people to abandon sin and adopt virtue, when they could have taken the fast-track to social salvation by condemning free exchange and private property.

What the great moralists knew, and we've forgotten, is that people and cultures are products of human choice. Good lives can flourish in any social setting, whether the prison camp, the Wild West or Washington, D.C. (hard as the latter is to believe).

Sin and stupidity will, of course, always be with us. From an economic perspective, our goal should be to make sure that sinners pay for their sins, and that minimal resources are used to cater to them. In this process, capitalism is our ally. In addition to making prosperity possible, the whole point of economics and markets is to make sure the minimum amount of resources is used to satisfy any particular demand of any particular group.

The free economy is efficient because it deals with tastes and preferences as a given, it organizes resources in an economically practical way, and it arranges for the consumer to get what he wants at the least possible cost to everyone else.

The junk on television may indeed speak volumes about our culture. People should care about more important things. Thanks to capitalism, however, society isn't wasting excess resources on it. Trash is delivered in the least costly manner,

From *The Free Market*, October 1995, Vol. 13, No. 10. Reprinted by permission of Ludwig von Mises Institute.

leaving more resources for the pursuit of what really matters.

Entrepreneurs have learned to provide services to even the smallest niche. When I see television, and I don't very often, the most intelligent network is EWTN. It features 50-part lectures by learned academics on subjects like Scholasticism.

This is a profitable enterprise that would be considered wasteful in a socialist country—not to mention politically incorrect. In a less prosperous society, it couldn't survive. Yet I can't remember anyone crediting capitalism for making St. Thomas Aquinas accessible the masses.

It used to be said that government had to fund the arts for them to be of good quality. That argument no longer flies. Take a look at the malevolent and stupid creations of the National Endowment for Arts. The government's "sculptures," "architecture," and "music" has littered the country with rubbish.

Economists say that the market "internalizes externalities." This means, in part, that people who are offended by some goods and services can structure their lives to avoid exposure. That's mostly true, especially in the case of sleazy television and movies, pornography, and weird services like telephone sex. Thanks to capitalism—which restricts such services to the people who purchase them—the rest of us don't have to be affected.

A shop selling occult trinkets recently opened up in Auburn, Alabama. "Anything for a buck," people sneered, until the store went belly-up for lack of business. It's true that some people *Will* for a buck, but in a market economy, they have to be subservient to the consuming public.

The market delivers plenty of similar good news, though most of it goes unremarked. Let's consider the case of big cities, which the productive public has beefy out of for decades.

The government has done everything in its power to make cities uninhabitable by regular people. Government welfare has fostered a whole class of citizens that is at once indolent and criminal. Public housing and rental subsidies have destroyed settings that were once middle-class. Many cities today are only "cultural" centers if you like freaks and muggers.

Yet, thanks to capitalism, there is hope. Private individuals and developers take buildings that appear beyond repair and revive them. House by house, block by block, whole sections of cities have been gentrified. It's not charity work. Without a system of profit and loss, it wouldn't happen.

Yet you can't satisfy those with an anti-capitalist mentality. They invariably complain that gentrification raises property values and "squeezes" out the poor, while forgetting to notice how much better off everyone is when degraded resources are made more valuable.

Beach housing has long been a magnet for cultural complaints against capitalism. High-rise buildings were routinely called evil for destroying the view from a mile away. Yet it is this type of structure which makes beach living possible for the masses in the first place.

Some architects, in revulsion against beach high rises, have worked with investors to buy miles of property on the beach. Then they create communities with quaint houses and shops. The result is magnificent, and entirely private, if affordable only for a few.

These architects tank they're repudiating the tackiness of capitalism. They fail to realize that their private, planned communities are as much a part of capitalism as the high rises. Far from making a left-wing ides point, they are catering to different tastes, marketing a product, and vastly increasing the value of property as a result. High rises and private communities represent capitalism at work.

The Nature of the Welfare State

Sheldon Richman

Welfare-state programs have three central characteristics: plunder, deception, and obfuscation. Because those programs always effect a forcible transfer of wealth from one group of individuals to another, they involve what the great 19th-century economist Frederic Bastiat called "legalized plunder." The law sanctions stealing in these cases and is thereby changed from its original purpose, which was to protect people's rights and property. Bastiat's classic book *The Law* explains this point with the utmost clarity.

Most people don't like to have their wealth taken away. (People are funny that way.) So if the government is to get away with legalized plunder, the politicians must make people believe that something else is going on. That's where the deception comes into play.

However, deception can be expected to work for only so long. People may stumble onto the facts and upset things. If the programs are to endure, the truth needs to be sufficiently obscured so that even if people try to take a close look, it won't be obvious what is happening. That's obfuscation. (Try to read any piece of legislation if you want to see how the people are kept from understanding what the government is doing.)

We can see this pattern almost everywhere. The federal budget is a monument to legalized plunder, deception, and obfuscation. The government is a great broker, arranging huge transfers of money from the mass of unorganized citizens to smaller, well-organized interests. Of course, the broker always gets his fee.

Besides being able to hide what they are doing, the policymakers and their clients have other advantages too. As the public-choice theorists have long taught, in the political arena the small, well-organized group almost always can have its way over the mass of citizens. That seems paradoxical in a democracy, where votes are supposed to count. In a country where sugar consumers far outnumber sugar producers, why is there a sugar program designed to keep sugar prices artificially high? That same question can be asked about any number of products and commodities. Why don't the users outvote the producers?

The paradox is resolved by the concepts of "dispersed costs" and "concentrated benefits." The price of any single government program, such as the sugar program, is small for any individual consumer. If he could compute the additional amount he has to pay because of the program, it would probably seem too small to justify active opposition. Most people are busy making a living and raising their families. The opportunity costs of organizing against the sugar program would outweigh the benefits even if there was a good chance the program could be abolished. A fully informed citizen would probably shrug his shoulders with regret and a sense of futility. That is the effect of dispersed costs.

While the expense to any individual is small, the total cost for all citizens is huge. That reverses the incentives for the relatively small group on the receiving end of the program. Those large benefits are divided among that small group. Since each member of the group stands to gain a great deal, it is worth his time to actively lobby for the program, or more precisely, to pay dues to a trade association that will set up shop in Washington, D.C., and look after his interests. That is the effect of concentrated benefits.

It is no mystery, then, that special interests prevail over the vast majority of citizens. Most of us have too little to gain materially from trying to stop individual welfare-state programs. Maybe that's what Thomas Jefferson had in mind when he said that there is a natural tendency for government to grow and for liberty to yield.

The process just discussed is enough to keep government programs going for a long time. But it is always possible that after a while, enough citizens could get so angry by the injustice of a welfare-state program that they actively oppose it even if the financial reward isn't large. In other words, ideology could outweigh mere material interest. In 19th-century England, Richard Cobden and John Bright got enough people angry about the tariff on foreign grain that their Anti-Corn Law League was able to have the tariff repealed before a decade had elapsed.

To prevent that, the designers of programs like to keep things from being too clear. Some plunder is obvious. With a straight cash subsidy, the government takes money from A and gives it to B. But more subtle methods can be used. Here is where deception and obfuscation enter. The citizens are told that there is no subsidy because not a penny of taxpayers' money goes to the special interest in question. That could be true, but it is deceptive. Many subsidies are not direct cash grants. They are indirect. For example, domestic sugar producers benefit from sugar prices that are kept artificially high by restrictions on imports through a system of quotas. Under free trade, domestic producers can't charge above-market prices because foreign producers are free to undersell them. Thus, an effective and subtle way to transfer wealth from citizens to particular domestic producers is to restrict imports. There is little real difference between that method of transferring wealth and directly taxing citizens for the benefit of those domestic interests. But the first method obscures what is really going on.

Incidentally, subsidies such as import restrictions can benefit other parties too, even more indirectly. Since sugar is artificially expensive under the sugar program, a market for other kinds of sweeteners, like high-fructose corn syrup, has emerged. Did you ever wonder why Archer-Daniels-Midland promotes the sugar program, when it is not a sugar producer? It is because the company makes corn syrup, which food manufacturers buy instead of expensive sugar.

There are other subtle ways of subsidizing special interests. Dairy interests are benefitted by a program under which the government promises to buy milk and cheese at an above-market price. If consumers won't pay the inflated price voluntarily, the government will force them to as taxpayers. Of course, the government must also tax the citizens to pay for the warehousing of the milk and cheese.

There is another piece of deception we should not ignore. Defenders of the programs can always be counted on to claim that the programs actually benefit the average citizen. The farm programs are sometimes defended as saving consumers from price fluctuations.

We can say without fear of contradiction that politicians, bureaucrats, and organized interests have been very clever in deceiving the American people and then obfuscating sufficiently so that few people discover what is happening. The public-choice scholars are correct in considering this process "political entrepreneurship." That's a perverse form of entrepreneurship in which people get wealthy by devising innovative ways to fleece consumers and taxpayers. One of the tragedies of the welfare state is that energy that might have gone into economic entrepreneurship and production for the benefit of everyone is instead diverted into political entrepreneurship, which restricts production and benefits a few.

If we analyze the programs of the welfare state, we will find to a greater or lesser extent the elements we've been discussing: plunder, deception, and obfuscation. This is easily seen with the crown jewel of the welfare state, Social Security. The working generation is plundered for the benefit of the retirees. The government deceives the workers by implying that the money is being saved for them and that it will be there when they retire. In fact, the government just plans to tax the next group of workers. The whole process is obfuscated with talk about trust funds and employer contributions. This last is especially egregious. Workers are led to believe that employers are kicking in half of the "contribution," which is actually a tax. That makes the system appear to be a good deal. In fact, the employer cannot really contribute. Anything he appears to pay is really part of the workers' compensation. Without Social Security, that cash would have been paid to them. The market sets pay levels. If the government commands employers to pay into Social Security in behalf of their workers, regular cash compensation will be reduced. There is no way around that fact. But the appearance of an employer contribution is a clever act of deception and obfuscation.

Bastiat long ago recognized the dishonesty at the foundation of the welfare state when he called it a great fiction whereby everyone tries to live at everyone else's expense. Perhaps the way to hasten the demise of the welfare state is to focus our teaching on how the system is in fact a big lie. Maybe that will awaken the American people in time.

An Environment Without Property Rights

Richard L. Stroup and Jane S. Shaw

When Eastern Europe began to open up in the late 1980s, one of the great shocks was the severity of its environmental problems. Journalists reported on skies full of smoke from lignite and soft coal, children kept inside for much of the winter because of unsafe air, and horses that had to be moved away from the worst areas after a few years or they would die.

Many of the environmental ills reflected an abysmally low level of technology. Old, polluting factories of the kinds that are dim memories in the United States were the mainstay of socialist industry. Smelly, sluggish automobiles polluted the roads.

Energy waste was tremendous. Their own statistics showed that socialist economies were using more than three times as much steel and nearly three times as much energy per unit of output than market economies.[1] One cannot look about in Warsaw or Moscow, Budapest or Zagreb, Krakow or Sarajevo, wrote economist W. W. Rostow in 1991, without knowing that this part of the world is caught up in a technological time warp.[2]

Not everyone realized it at the time, but the state of the environment was directly connected to the absence of property rights in the Soviet system. The authorities had refused to allow most resources to be privately owned. Most market exchanges were criminal acts, and entrepreneurship of most kinds was declared to be criminal behavior. Production was centrally planned, with land and other resources owned by the state, not individuals.

Although there were many repressive acts in the former Soviet Union and the Eastern European nations, the absence of property rights, along with the absence of the markets that result from the exchange of property rights, was enough to devastate the environment.

To understand why, it is helpful to look at the reasons why private property rights protect the environment. There are several:[3]

1. Owners have incentives to use resources productively and to conserve where possible. Owners can obtain financial rewards from using resources productively and they have a strong incentive to reduce costs by conserving on their use of each resource. In the pursuit of profits, business firms have a strong incentive to implement new resource-saving technologies.

Such incentives were absent in the Eastern bloc under socialism. Consider the Trabant, the people's car produced in East Germany between 1959 and 1989.[4] (Production stopped shortly after the Berlin Wall came down.)

The Trabant provided basic transportation and was easy to fix. But it was slow (top speed 66 mph), noisy, it had no discernible handling, it spewed a plume of oil and gray exhaust smoke, and it didn't have a gas gauge. The exhaust was so noxious that West Germans were not allowed to own Trabants. When the magazine Car and Driver brought one to the United States, the EPA refused to let it be driven on public streets.

The Trabant was so bad partly because its design was basically the same as it had been when the car was first manufactured in 1959. The latest model, the 601, had been introduced in 1964, and was essentially unchanged 25 years later.

Manufacturers could not reap a profit from making a better car, so they had no incentive to adopt new, cleaner technology that would give better performance. Indeed, because factories were government-owned, there was little incentive to produce any cars at all in East Germany. So few automobiles were available that people waited an average of 13 years to get their Trabant.

2. Private ownership of property provides an incentive for good care that is lacking under government control. If a resource is well cared for, it will be

more valuable and add more to the personal wealth of its owner. If the owner allows the resource to deteriorate or be harmed by pollution, he or she personally bears the cost of that negligence in the form of a decline in the value of the resource.

Throughout the Soviet Union under Communism, resources were routinely wasted. In fact, the emphasis was on using up resources, not on producing them—for a good reason. Central planners often measured the use of inputs to determine whether a factory or other entity was carrying out the central plan. For example, Ann-Mari Satre Ahlander reports that despite the low per capita production of agricultural crops, the use of fertilizers and herbicides was high.[5] That is because using them was a sign that work was being done, even though excessive use of these chemicals could have harmful effects.

A story is told about a part of Estonia where the underground water is flammable because vast quantities of aviation fuel were dumped into the ground and they seeped into the water. The fuel was assigned to a nearby Soviet military station to be used for flying practice missions. To make sure that the pilots had flown the required number of hours, the military superiors monitored the amount of fuel the pilots used. When the pilots did not want to fly the required hours, they falsified their reports. To evade detection, they got rid of the fuel by dumping it onto the ground.[6]

3. A resource owner has legal rights against anyone who would harm the resource. The private owner of a resource has more than just the incentive to preserve the value of that resource. Private property rights also provide the owner with legal rights against anyone (usually including a government agency) who invades—physically or by pollution—and harms the resource. The private owner of a forest or a farm will not sit idly by if someone is cutting down trees without permission or invading the property with hazardous pollutants, and lawsuits can be used to protect those rights. A private owner could probably have stopped the dumping of aviation fuel on the Estonian farmland mentioned above.

But in the Eastern bloc, such protection was absent. Peter J. Hill reports that in Bulgaria heavy metals in irrigation water lowered crop yields on Bulgarian farms. The industrial sources of the metals were known, but the farmers had no recourse. Without a system of redress through the courts, says Hill, the farmers had no actionable claim against those causing the problems.[7]

4. Property rights provide long-term incentives for maximizing the value of a resource, even for owners whose personal outlook is short-term. If using a tract of land for the construction of a toxic waste dump reduces its future productivity, its value falls today, reducing the owner's wealth. That happens because land's current worth reflects the net present value of its future services—the revenue from production or services received directly from the land, minus the costs required to generate the revenues (and both discounted to present value terms).

Lake Baikal is the largest and deepest freshwater lake on Earth. Once known for its purity, it is now heavily polluted because Soviet planners decided to build paper mills at its edge and failed to reduce the emission of pollutants into the water. According to one source, the effluent is discharged directly into the lake and has created a polluted area 23 miles wide.[8] Clearly, the value of the lake and its surrounding land has been seriously diminished by pollution.

PART

VI

Economic Articles

Part VI

- Capitalism and the Common Man
- Why Socialism Failed
- What To Do About Recession
- CNN money economic articles two
  1. Greenspan Backs China Bill. May 18, 2000
  2. P.R. on the rise in China. June 14, 2002
- Consumer Axiety Puts Dow in Dive
- GDP on Solid Growth Plan
- Greenspan: Soaring Budget Deficits Represent Long-Term Threat

Capitalism and the Common Man

Walter E. Williams

There are some arguments, having a faint measure of plausibility, that have served politicians, charlatans, and assorted do-gooders for well over a century in their quest for control. One of those arguments is: capitalism primarily benefits the rich and not the common man. That vision prompts declarations such as Representative Richard Gephardt's assertion that high-income earners are "winners" in "the lottery of life." Then there's Robert Reich, former secretary of labor, who calls high-income earners the "fortunate fifth." This nonsensical vision leads to calls for those who've been "blessed" to "give back" either voluntarily or coercively through the tax code.

While demagogic statements like these have high emotive worth, they reflect resolute, nearly incurable stupidity about the sources of income. Listening to some of the talk about income differences, one would think that out there somewhere is a pile of money. People who are wealthy just happened to get there first and greedily took an unfair share. Justice requires that they give back. Or there's talk about unequal income distribution. The way some people talk, you'd think there's a dealer of dollars who shells out $1,000 to one person, $100,000 to another, and a million dollars to yet another. Thus the reason why some people are wealthy while others are not wealthy is that the dollar dealer is a racist, sexist, or multi-nationalist—or just plain mean. Economic justice requires a redealing of the dollars, income redistribution, where the ill-gotten gains of the few are returned to their rightful owners.

In a free society, for the most part, people with high incomes have demonstrated extra-ordinary ability to produce valuable services for, and therefore to please, their fellow man. Sam Walton, founder of Wal-Mart; Bill Gates, founder of Microsoft; and singer Michael Jackson provided services deemed highly valuable by their fellow men who voluntarily took money out of their pocket to purchase those services. Their high incomes stand as unambiguous proof of that service. Their high incomes also reflect the "democracy" of the marketplace. For example, millions upon millions of independent decision-makers decided to fork over $200 for Gates's Windows 98 operating system. Those who think Gates is too rich and want to redistribute his income are really registering disagreement with the "democracy" of the marketplace and want to cancel or offset the market "vote."

Indeed, we might consider the dollars people earn as certificates of performance. Think of it in the following way. You hire me to mow your lawn. After I have completed the task, you give me $20. I go to the grocer and demand a pound of steak and a six-pack of beer that my fellow man produced. The grocer says, "You're demanding something that your fellow man has produced. What have you done to serve him?" I reply, "I have served my fellow man by moving his lawn." The grocer says, "Prove it!" That's when I hand him my $20, my certificate of performance.

Income earners owe nothing else to their fellow man; they have met their social obligations. If "giving something back" means anything, it should be the admonition to thieves and social parasites: people who have taken and given nothing in return. We have it backwards. Highly productive (rich) people like Walton and Gates are held up to social ridicule, while thieves and bums are shown compassion and concern and have become society's mascots.

Good for the Masses

Capitalism is the best thing that every happened to the common man. The rich have always had access to entartainment, often in the comfort of their palaces and mansions. The rich have never had to experience the drudgery of beating out carpets, ironing their clothing, or slaving over a hot stove all day to have a decent dinner; they could afford to hire people. Capitalism's mass production and marketing have made radios and televisions, vacuum cleaners, wash-and-wear clothing, and microwave ovens available and well within the means of the common man, sparing him the boredom and drudgery of the past. Today the common man has the power to enjoy more than what only the rich had yesteryear.

What about those who became wealthy making comforts available to the common man? Henry Ford benefited immensely from mass-producing automobiles, but the benefit for the common man from being able to buy a car dwarfs anything Ford received. Individuals and companies that produced penicillin and polio and typhoid vaccines may have become very wealthy, but again it was the common man who was the major beneficiary. In more recent times, computers and software products have benefited our health, safety, and quality of life in ways that far outstrip whatever wealth was received by their creators.

Here's a little test. Stand on the corner and watch people walk or drive by. Then, based on their appearances, identify which persons are wealthy. Years ago, that wouldn't have been a difficult challenge. Ordinary people wouldn't be dressed as well, surely not wearing designer clothing, nor would they have nice-looking jewelry. They wouldn't be driving by. Compare the income status of today's airline passengers with those of a few years ago and you'll find a much greater percentage of ordinary people.

That's one of the great benefits of capitalism; it has made it possible for common people to enjoy at least some of what wealthy people enjoy. One might assert that common people don't have access to Rolls Royces and yachts. You're wrong. Gates is super-rich and can afford to ride in a Rolls Royce and go yachting; but so can the common man—just not as long. He can rent a Rolls or a yacht for a day, a half-day, or an hour.

Capitalism is relatively new in human history. Before the rise of capitalism, the way people amassed wealth was by looting, plundering, and enslaving their fellow man. Capitalism made it possible to become wealthy be serving one's fellow man. Capitalists seek to discover what people want and then produce and market it as efficiently as possible.

Here's a question that we should ponder: are the wealthy people who have created unprecedented convenience, longer life expectancy, and more fun for the ordinary person deserving of all the scorn and ridicule heaped on them by intellectuals and politicians? Are the wealthy really obliged to "give something back"? Exactly what more do the wealthy discoverers and producers of, say, life-saving antibiotics owe us? They've already saved lives and made us healthier.

Despite the miracles of capitalism, it doesn't do sell in popularity polls. One reason is that capitalism is always evaluated against the non-existent, unrealizable utopias of socialism or communism. Any earthly system will pale in comparison to a utopia. But for the ordinary person, capitalism, with all of its warts, is superior to any system devised to deal with our everyday needs and desires.

Why Socialism Failed

Mark J. Perry

Socialism is the Big Lie of the twentieth century. While it promised prosperity, equality, and security, it delivered poverty, misery, and tyranny. Equality was achieved only in the sense that everyone was equal in his or her misery.

In the same way that a Ponzi scheme or chain letter initially succeeds but eventually collapses, socialism may show early signs of success. But any accomplishments quickly fade as the fundamental deficiencies of central planning emerge. It is the initial illusion of success that gives government intervention its pernicious, seductive appeal. In the long run, socialism has always proven to be a formula for tyranny and misery.

A pyramid scheme is ultimately unsustainable because it is based on faulty principles. Likewise, collectivism is unsustainable in the long run because it is a flawed theory. Socialism does not work because it is not consistent with fundamental principles of human behavior. The failure of socialism in countries around the world can be traced to one critical defect: it is a system that ignores incentives.

In a capitalist economy, incentives are of the utmost importance. Market prices, the profit-and-loss system of accounting, and private property rights provide an efficient, interrelated system of incentives to guide and direct economic behavior. Capitalism is based on the theory that incentives matter!

Under socialism, incentives either play a minimal role or are ignored totally. A centrally planned economy without market prices or profits, where property is owned by the state, is a system without an effective incentive mechanism to direct economic activity. By falling to emphasize incentives, socialism is a theory inconsistent with human nature and is therefore doomed to fail. Socialism is based on the theory that incentives don't matter!

In a radio debate several months ago with a Marxist professor from the University of Minnesota, I pointed out the obvious failures of socialism around the world in Cuba, Eastern Europe, and China. At the time of our debate, Haitian refugees were risking their lives trying to get to Florida in homemade boats. Why was it, I asked him, that people were fleeing Haiti and traveling almost 500 miles by ocean to get to the "evil capitalist empire" when they were only 50 miles from the "workers' paradise" of Cuba?

The Marxist admitted that many "socialist" countries around the world were failing. However, according to him, the reason for failure is not that socialism is deficient, but that the socialist economies are not practicing "pure" socialism. The perfect version of socialism would work; it is just the imperfect socialism that doesn't work. Marxists like to compare a theoretically perfect version of socialism with practical, imperfect capitalism which allows them to claim that socialism is superior to capitalism.

If perfection really were an available option, the choice of economic and political systems would be irrelevant. In a world with perfect beings and infinite abundance, any economic or political system—socialism, capitalism, fascism, or communism—would work perfectly.

However, the choice of economic and political institutions is crucial in an imperfect universe with imperfect beings and limited resources. In a world of scarcity it is essential for an economic system to be based on a clear incentive structure to promote economic efficiency. The real choice we face is between imperfect capitalism and imperfect socialism. Given that choice, the evidence of history overwhelmingly favors capitalism as the greatest wealth-producing economic system available.

The strength of capitalism can be attributed to an incentive structure based upon the three Ps: (1) prices determined by market forces, (2) a profit-and-loss system of accounting and (3) private property rights. The failure of socialism can be traced to its neglect of these three incentive-enhancing components.

Prices

The price system in a market economy guides economic activity so flawlessly that most people don't appreciate its importance. Market prices transmit information about relative scarcity and then efficiently coordinate economic activity. The economic content of prices provides incentives that promote economic efficiency.

For example, when the OPEC cartel restricted the supply of oil in the 1970s, oil prices rose dramatically. The higher prices for oil and gasoline transmitted valuable information to both buyers and sellers. Consumers received a strong, clear message about the scarcity of oil by the higher prices at the pump and were forced to change their behavior dramatically. People reacted to the scarcity by driving less, carpooling more, taking public transportation, and buying smaller cars. Producers reacted to the higher price by increasing their efforts at exploration for more oil. In addition, higher oil prices gave producers an incentive to explore and develop alternative fuel and energy sources.

The information transmitted by higher oil prices provided the appropriate incentive structure to both buyers and sellers. Buyers increased their effort to conserve a now more precious resource and sellers increased their effort to find more of this now scarcer resource.

The only alternative to a market price is a controlled or fixed price which always transmits misleading information about relative scarcity. Inappropriate behavior results from a controlled price because false information has been transmitted by an artificial, non-market price.

Look at what happened during the 1970s when U.S. gas prices were controlled. Long lines developed at service stations all over the country because the price for gasoline was kept artificially low by government fiat. The full impact of scarcity was not accurately conveyed. As Milton Friedman pointed out at the time, we could have eliminated the lines at the pump in one day by allowing the price to rise to clear the market.

From our experience with price controls on gasoline and the long lines at the pump and general inconvenience, we get an insight into what happens under socialism where every price in the economy is controlled. The collapse of socialism is due in part to the chaos and inefficiency that result from artificial prices. The information content of a controlled price is always distorted. This in turn distorts the incentives mechanism of prices under socialism. Administered prices are always either too high or too law, which then creates constant shortages and surpluses. Market prices are the only way to transmit information that will create the incentives to ensure economic efficiency.

Profits and Losses

Socialism also collapsed because of its failure to operate under a competitive, profit-and-loss system of accounting. A profit system is an effective monitoring mechanism which continually evaluates the economic performance of every business enterprise. The firms that are the most efficient and most successful at serving the public interest are rewarded with profits. Firms that operate inefficiently and fail to serve the public interest are penalized with losses.

By rewarding success and penalizing failure, the profit system provides a strong disciplinary mechanism which continually redirects resources away from weak, failing, and inefficient firms toward those firms which are the most efficient and successful at serving the public. A competitive profit system ensures a constant reoptimization of resources and moves the economy toward greater levels of efficiency. Unsuccessful firms cannot escape the strong discipline of the marketplace under a profit/loss system. Competition forces companies to serve the public interest or suffer the consequences.

Under central planning, there is no profit-and-loss system of accounting to accurately measure the success or failure of various programs. Without profits, there is no way to discipline firms that fail to serve the public interest and no way to reward firms that do. There is no efficient way to determine which programs should be expanded and which ones should be contracted or terminated.

Without competition, centrally planned economies do not have an effective incentive structure to coordinate economic activity. Without incentives the results are a spiraling cycle of poverty and misery. Instead of continually reallocating resources towards greater efficiency, socialism falls into a vortex of inefficiency and failure.

Private Property Rights

A third fatal defect of socialism is its blatant disregard for the role of private property rights in creating incentives that foster economic growth and development. The failure of socialism around the world is a "tragedy of commons" on a global scale.

The "tragedy of the commons" refers to the British experience of the sixteenth century when certain grazing lands were communally owned by villages and were made available for public use. The land was quickly overgrazed and eventually became worthless as villagers exploited the communally owned resource.

When assets are publicly owned, there are no incentives in place to encourage wise stewardship. While private property creates incentives for conservation and the responsible use of property, public property encourages irresponsibility and waste. If everyone owns an asset, people act as if no one owns it. And when no one owns it, no one really takes care of it. Public ownership encourages neglect and mismanagement.

Since socialism by definition, is a system marked by the "common ownership of the means of production," the failure of socialism is a "tragedy of the commons" on a national scale. Much of the economic stagnation of socialism can be traced to the failure to establish and promote private property rights.

As Peruvian economist Hernando de Soto remarked, you can travel in rural communities around the world and you will hear dogs barking, because even dogs understand property rights. It is only statist governments that have failed to understand property rights. Socialist countries are just now starting to recognize the importance of private property as they privatize assets and property in Eastern Europe.

Incentives Matter

Without the incentives of market prices, profit-and-loss accounting, and well-defined property rights, socialist economies stagnate and wither. The economic atrophy that occurs under socialism is a direct consequence of its neglect of economic incentives.

No bounty of natural resources can ever compensate a country for its lack of an efficient system of incentives. Russia, for example, is one of the world's wealthiest countries in terms of natural resources; it has some of the world's largest reserves of oil, natural gas, diamonds, and gold. Its valuable farm land, lakes, rivers, and streams stretch across a land area that encompasses 11 time zones. Yet Russia remains poor. Natural resources are helpful, but the ultimate resources of any country are the unlimited resources of its people—human resources.

By their failure to foster, promote, and nurture the potential of their people through incentive-enhancing institutions, centrally planned economies deprive the human spirit of full development. Socialism fails because it kills and destroys the human spirit—just ask the people leaving Cuba in homemade rafts and boats.

As the former centrally planned economies move toward free markets, capitalism, and democracy, they look to the United States for guidance and support during the transition. With an unparalleled 250-year tradition of open markets and limited government, the United States is uniquely qualified to be the guiding light in the worldwide transition to freedom and liberty.

We have an obligation to continue to provide a framework of free markets and democracy for the global transition to freedom. Our responsibility to the rest of the world is to continue to fight the seductiveness of statism around the world and here at home. The seductive nature of statism continues to tempt and lure us into the Barmecidal illusion that the government can create wealth.

The temptress of socialism is constantly luring us with the offer: "give up a little of your freedom and I will give you a little more security." As the experience of this century has demonstrated, the bargain is tempting but never pays off. We end up losing both our freedom and our security.

Programs like socialized medicine, welfare, social security, and minimum wage laws will continue to entice us because on the surface they appear to be expedient and beneficial. Those programs, like all socialist programs, will fail in the long run regardless of initial appearance. These programs are part of the Big Lie of socialism because they ignore the important role of incentives.

Socialism will remain a constant temptation. We must be vigilant in our fight against socialism not only around the globe but also here in the United States.

The failure of socialism inspired a worldwide renaissance of freedom and liberty. For the first time in the history of the world, the day is coming very soon when a majority of the people in the world will live in free societies or societies rapidly moving towards freedom.

Capitalism will play a major role in the global revival of liberty and prosperity because it nurtures the human spirit, inspires human creativity, and promotes the spirit of enterprise. By providing a powerful system of incentives that promote thrift, hard work, and efficiency, capitalism creates wealth.

The main difference between capitalism and socialism is this: Capitalism works.

What To Do About the Recession

William L. Anderson

With the latest news that the U.S. economy officially has been shrinking, it is time to admit the obvious: We are in a recession. Consumer spending is down, along with business investment. The only people making money these days are those who contract with the Pentagon.

Some are claiming that the attacks of September 11 triggered this latest economic slide, but all signs point to the fact that the U.S. economy already was in the recession even before the attacks. Moreover, there is no scarcity of counsel to be given to those we are told are "in charge" of the economy, as though there are a few people who can just pull the right levers to make things work. For the most part, we hear the pundits telling everyone else what must be done to "stimulate" the economy in order to drive it from the doldrums. Good luck.

Actually, I would like to give some advice of my own to the august chairman of the Federal Reserve System, Mr. Greenspan: Quit, and close down your whole operation. You will not be missed.

Of course, that is not what we are hearing from the pundits. Instead, the word from nearly all quarters is for the Fed to continue to cut interest rates, which it has already done on numerous occasions, with the results being that the economy still falters. We also hear calls for new tax cuts that should be targeted to people who would "spend money" and thus "stimulate" the economy.

As an Austrian economist, I am always for tax cuts and more tax cuts, because lower taxes mean a smaller state. However, to say that the chief purpose of government policy is to "stimulate" the economy is to engage in silly talk. For all its alleged great powers, the government cannot stop this recession. The government and its wrongheaded policies are responsible for this economic calamity, not the hijackers who murdered several thousand people, as dreadful as that act was. (No doubt, even if the economy were strong, U.S. productivity would be down in the wake of such a terrible event.) The problem is simple: Bad ideas are leading to bad policies.

American economists like to think of themselves as a sophisticated lot, but to read their numerous policy prescriptions gives further proof that few in that profession have progressed beyond Bernard de Mandeville's *The Fable of the Bees, or Private Vices Public Benefits.* The difference between the admonitions given by someone like Paul Krugman in the *New York Times* and Mandeville in *Fable of the Bees* is that Mandeville was a better writer. For that matter, "I Want to be a Consumer," which appeared in the April 25, 1934, edition of *Punch,* describes the Keynesian fallacies even better than Keynes and Krugman could do themselves. At least the editors of *Punch* realized that "stimulating" consumption was a joke, while Krugman takes Keynesianism quite seriously.

Despite the fact that Keynesian "theory" has been discredited time and again, it always makes a comeback. The only point of argument these days seems to be what kind of "stimulus" the economy requires, as opposed to why this business-cycle bust has happened in the first place. Until people understand why we are in recession and what must be done for the economy to climb out and avoid this problem in the future, we are doomed to repeat these failures time and again.

First, repeat after me: Greenspan did not cause this recession by raising interest rates in 2000. That is correct. Instead, Greenspan helped cause this recession by *lowering* interest rates during the late 1990s. To put it another way, Greenspan's "cure" to fight business-cycle downturns is actually responsible for the problem it was trying to correct.

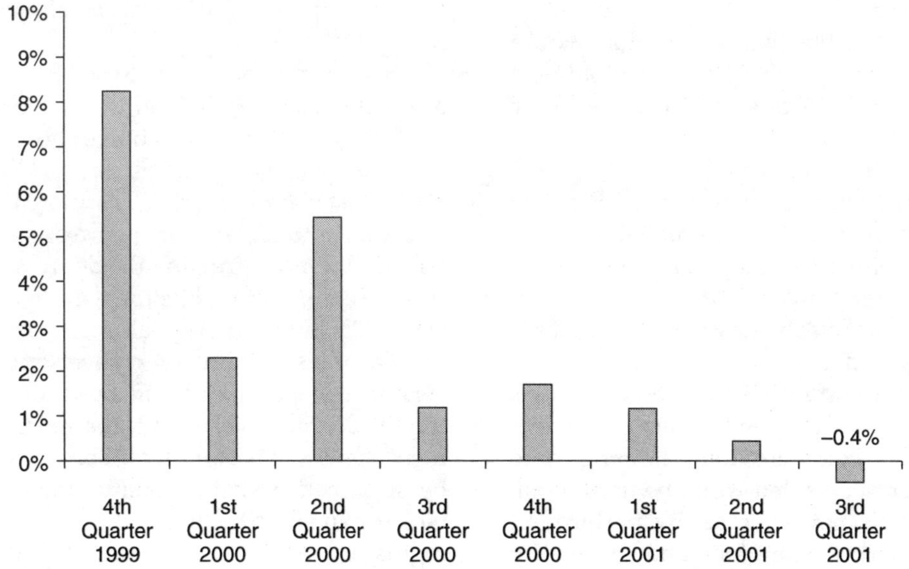

Gross Domestic Product
Source: Department of Commerce.

Conventional wisdom goes as follows: the health of the economy directly depends upon aggregate demand. If consumers are confident and secure, they will spend money and the economy will flourish. However, if consumers lose confidence or if they believe the future to be uncertain, then they will withhold some spending and drive the economy into recession. Thus, we have been hearing articles about the "heroic consumer" who was supposedly propping up the economy until losing heart after the September 11 attacks. The terrorists who destroyed the World Trade Towers and damaged the Pentagon committed murder and mayhem; however, they are *not guilty* of causing a recession that was already inevitable. Greenspan did just fine on his own, thank you.

Second, in order to "stimulate" the economy, we must rebate tax dollars to consumers so they will spend it quickly; so say the Keynesians. At this point, people on the "right" and "left" disagree who should be the main beneficiaries of tax cuts. So-called conservatives argue that cuts in capital gains taxes and of high marginal income tax rates will stimulate investment, while leftists hold that lower-income people should receive most of the cuts, since they are likely to spend money instead of saving or investing it like upper-income individuals might do.

While Austrians obviously would be more sympathetic to the former proposal than the latter, most people involved in the current public discussion of economics actually are clueless about what causes business cycles. Furthermore, their ignorance of the reason economies run through boom-and-bust cycles blinds them to the real damage done by government policies, regardless of which political party holds power.

Although I agree that the government should slash tax rates, I believe so out of a matter of principle, not because I believe that government has the power to "stimulate" private investment. That the economy is in recession in the first place is testament to the policy failures of the U.S. government.

In going back to an earlier statement, let me say again that the inevitability of this current recession began when the Fed began to force down interest rates during the mid-1990s. The Fed's actions had a major role in triggering a boom, especially in the high-technology sector of the economy. As the boom continued, it was fed by artificially low interest rates and a false belief that we had entered a "new economy" in which business cycles were a thing of the past.

Austrian economists—and only the Austrians—were pointing out that the boom was not a new era of prosperity that had been created by former President Bill Clinton's 1993 tax increases or Secretary of the Treasury Robert Rubin's brilliant business strategies. While we need to acknowledge that some of the business, transportation, and financial "deregulation" (or re-regulation) of the late 1970s and early 1980s improved the basic climate for business investment, the Greenspan-led boom created an atmosphere in which billions of dollars became malinvested into lines of production that could not be sustained, especially in the high-technology and Internet sectors.

Once those malinvestments took place on a huge scale, it became inevitable that a recession would occur. To put it another way, there was no avoiding a bust, once those billions of dollars found their way into unsustainable lines of production.

What about the present efforts of the Fed to stave off the recession by lowering interest rates? For one, those malinvestments that once responded to lower interest rates have either been liquidated or are not looking to borrow large sums of money. Thus, at best, this effort by the Fed to create massive new amounts of bank reserves is ineffective.

However, it is doubtful that we can easily walk away from this newest mess that Greenspan has created. Would that the Fed were doing nothing more than creating new reserves that won't be used at all. Unfortunately, that is not the case. By performing aggressive open market operations and by forcing interest rates below the rate of inflation, all of which are increasing the U.S. money supply at very high rates, the Fed is basically setting the stage for the next wave of malinvestments—even before investors have had the opportunity to malinvest their funds!

What should be the proper response, given all that the Fed and the U.S. government have done to cause this calamity? Murray N. Rothbard, in his classic *America's Great Depression,* eloquently answers that question:

If government wishes to see a depression ended as quickly as possible, and the economy returned to normal prosperity, what course should it adopt? The first and clearest injunction is: *don't interfere with the market's adjustment process.* The more the government intervenes to delay the market's adjustment, the longer and more grueling the depression will be, and the more difficult will be the road to complete recovery. (p. 25, italics in original.)

The prescription for recovery could hardly be clearer. Yes, cut taxes to the bone, because the lower the burden of government, the more private investment there will be, and it will be investment that can be sustained, not the malinvestments triggered by Greenspan and his allies at the Fed. Furthermore, the regulatory state we have created should be cut back severely or, even better, abolished altogether.

This recession does not have to last for a long time. We have the tools in hand to drastically shorten this economic downturn. It is just that most people don't know where to look or, instead, are mistakenly trying to use tools that caused the trouble in the first place.

Greespan Backs China Bill

Fed Chief Says Open Trade Is Best Way to Promote Human Rights, Economies

NEW YORK (CNNfn) - Federal Reserve Chairman Alan Greenspan urged a divided U.S. Congress Thursday to approve a bill expanding trade relations with China, saying the measure would benefit both countries' economies.

Greespan, in a rare endorsement of a pending bill before Congress, appeared at a White House event with President Clinton to press lawmakers to grant China permanent normal trade relations status. In exchange for the upgrade in trade relations, China would cut tariffs on U.S. imports and open a wide range of markets to American businesses.

Greenspan, a long-tim supporter of easing trade barriers, said the measure would raise standards of living in China, promoting internal economic development and encouraging the communist country to foster greater individual rights.

The measure also is vital U.S. interests, he said. "As China's citizens experience economic gains, so will the American firms that trade in their expanding markets," he said, reading from a letter that he had previously sent to the House Banking Committee supporting the trade accord.

Approval of the bill is a key step for China in its quest to join the World Trade Organization, the 135-nation body that sets world trade rules.

"China's progress towards prosperity and accession into the WTO will create new opportunities for American businesses and farmers," Greenspan said.

Greenspan said China currently accounts for 3 percent of world trade, a figure that is expected to jump if the country of 1.2 billion people becomes part of the WTO.

"Our markets are already generally open to China, and that will not be altered by PNTR [permanent normal trade relations]," the Fed chief said. "Passage of PNTR, however, will facilitate a further opening of China's markets to U.S. producers."

Critics of the legislation include human rights advocates and organized labor, which contends that U.S. companies will be tempted to shift work to low-wage plants in China, endangering U.S. jobs.

Supporters Confident of Passage

The House of Representatives is expected to vote on the PNTR legislation next week, with the vote considered too close to call.

The bill, however, got a boost Thursday as Republican congressional leaders announced a bipartisan agreement on companion legislation that would set up a watchdog commission to monitor human rights in China, a breakthrough that could sway some undecided lawmakers to vote for the measure.

"We're going to win this vote next week," California Rep. David Dreler, chief vote counter for the Republicans, told Reuters.

However, opponents of the bill condemned the monitoring plan and said they believed they had enough votes to defeat the bill.

"We don't need another commission. What we need is action. What we need is pressure. What we need is enforcement and action," said David Bonior, D-Mich., a leading opponent of the measure and the No. 2 House Democrat.

The Senate, which will take up the matter next month, is expected to approve the measure easily.

U.S. Treasury Secretary Lawrence Summers also stands firmly behind the trade deal with China. He told CNNfn that China's accession into the WTO would grant U.S. exporters an open market in the communist nation.

Meanwhile, President Clinton plans to address the nation Sunday evening from the Oval Office in an effort to build support for the bill, White House Press Secretary Joe Lockhart said. The address will start at 7 P.M. ET, last about five minutes and focus on the "Importance" of the issue for U.S. national security, Lockhart said.

In addition to passage of the trade bill in Congress, China faces another hurdle—hammering out a bilateral trade pact with the European Union. Talks between the two sides in Beijing came up short again Thursday, but negotiators agreed to resume discussions Friday.

The EU is the last major trade partner with China yet to reach a bilateral accord on WTO membership.

P.R. on the Rise in China

Lisa Barron

HONG KONG, China (CNN)—Public relations is on the rise in China as a growing number of international companies expand into the mainland and position themselves to tap its vast market.

Telco giant Nokia set the scene when it launched a P.R. campaign in Beijing last month linking its high-end mobile phone with an appreciation of traditional Chinese culture. The campaign is part of marketing its newest handset model in China.

Overseas companies are looking for good exposure in China, now that the country has entered the World Trade Organization. As a result, China's public relations market may be worth as much as $240 million a year.

Last week, Ogilvy Public Relations Worldwide acquired a Chinese communications firm to create the biggest P.R. group in China.

Ogilvy said it bought a majority stake in a joint venture with Beijing-based H-Line Public Relations. An overseas company is required to partner with a local company to operate in China.

"This will be the beginning of more investment into China. In the past, international firms have been too international and what we've seen is the opportunity to become rooted in the local market," said Matthew Anderson, president of Ogilvy P.R. Asia Pacific.

Two-Way Street

But the P.R. boom is not a one-way street. Chinese companies are also keen to position themselves internationally.

In the past, many companies in China did not have dedicated staff to handle queries from the press or public. Companies also had little incentive to market themselves strongly under the state-owned enterprise system.

But when Chinese oil giant CNOOC sought a dual listing on the Nasdaq and the Hong Kong Stock Exchange, it turned to international P.R. agency Weber Shandwick.

"We see more and more Chinese companies becoming more sophisticated in the way they approach P.R., with the type of firms they're looking to hire for P.R., because they want to tap overseas markets," says Emma Smith, co-president of Asia Pacific for Weber Shandwick.

This trend is spurring the growth of local P.R. firms, up 40 percent last year.

But the biggest P.R. coup to come out of China is Beijing's successful bid for the 2008 Olympics.

Determined not to repeat the loss of face when the 2000 Olympic Games were awarded to Sydney. China's Olympic bid committee hired Shandwick to take its case to the world.

Shandwick expects its business to grow 200–300 percent in China in the next few years. It will hire more local staff in the process.

"We see that the caliber of staff is really increasing," Smith says. "The levels of English, the levels of know-how, how to do work."

Consumer Anxiety Puts Dow in Dive

Blue Chip Stocks Lowest in 4 years

Ina Paiva Cordle

Low consumer confidence, disappointing earnings and a criminal investigation of Xerox's accounting practices led to a rough Tuesday on Wall Street, sending the Dow Jones industrials down nearly 190 points to hit a four-year low.

A Federal Reserve decision to keep overnight interest rates stable caused little market reaction, analysts said, but growing concerns about a possible war with Iraq worsened the selling.

"The market is trading on its own momentum," said Steven Eber, president of Eber Capital Management in Coral Gables. "The buyers have gone basically into a holding pattern, and the sellers are dominating."

On Wall Street, the Dow Jones industrial average fell 189.02 Tuesday, or 2.4 percent, to close at 7,683.13. The blue chips registered their fourth triple-digit loss in six sessions, falling to their lowest close since Oct. 1, 1998, when the average stood at 7,632.50. The Dow also broke through its 2002 low of 7,702.34, reached July 23.

The broader market also finished lower. The Nasdaq composite index dropped 2.76. or 0.2 percent, to 1,182.17, another six-year low. The Standard & Poor's 500 index was down 14.41, or 1.7 percent, at 819.29.

Uncertainty about jobs depressed consumer confidence in September to its lowest level in 10 months, raising new questions about consumers' willingness to spend in the coming months.

Lowest Level

The Conference Board said Tuesday that its Consumer Confidence Index fell for the fourth consecutive month, to 93.3 from a revised 94.5 in August. It was the lowest level since November. Analysts had expected a reading of 92.4. The industry group's index, based on a monthly survey of about 5,000 U.S. households, is closely watched because consumer confidence determines consumer spending. And consumer spending accounts for about two-thirds of the nation's economic activity.

"What consumers are telling us is that they feel uncomfortable about safety and politics and a war, not just about economics," said John Silvia, chief economist with Wachovia Securities.

Buy Lynn Franco, director of the Conference Board's Consumer Research Center, said consumers surveyed seemed to be preoccupied with jobs, not the threat of war.

On Tuesday, the Federal Reserve left a key interest rate unchanged. The Fed's decision to hold the federal funds rate steady means that commercial banks' prime lending rate— the benchmark for many loans—will remain at 4.75 percent, the lowest level since November 1965.

Fed Action

While the Fed held short-term interest rates steady, it continued to leave the door open to future rate reductions if economic conditions worsen. Two Fed members of 12 voted against keeping rates unchanged. They wanted to see the funds rate lowered.

"The choice was not between those who said, 'No' and those who said 'Yes.' " said Leo Guzman, president of Guzman & Co. in Miami. "It was between those who said, 'Yes,' and those who said, 'Not yet.' "

By keeping rates low or possibly nudging them down later, Fed policy-makers hope to motivate consumers to spend more and businesses to ramp up investment, something that would strengthen the fragile recovery.

Businesses have remained reluctant to make big commitments in hiring and capital spending, two factors restraining the recovery. Manufacturing—hardest hit by the recession—lost considerable momentum in August.

Layoffs have been rising recently, and economists are predicting that the nation's jobless rate—now at 5.7 percent—will probably increase slightly in the months ahead.

Consumers, whose spending accounts for two-thirds of all economic activity in the United States, have been the primary engine keeping the economy going.

They have taken advantage of free-financing deals to buy automobiles and home appliances. And low interest rates have motivated them to buy homes at such a brisk pace experts predict both sales of new and existing homes will set records this year.

Positive Factors

Low interest rates, good deals, rising home values and extra cash coming from a refinancing boom all are helping to support consumer spending.

Thus far, those positive factors have offset some potentially negative ones, including the volatile stock market, the lackluster job market and eroding consumer confidence.

Stock decliners on Tuesday included Xerox, which fell 71 cents to $5.96 after the company said federal prosecutors were opening a criminal inquiry into the company's accounting practices.

The airline sector also took a hit.

United Airlines' parent, UAL, fell 22 cents to $2.12, while AMR Corp. (American Airlines) dropped 62 cents to $3.60.

This report was supplemented with material from The Associated Press.

GDP on Solid Growth Path

A Report Showing Solid First-Quarter Growth of 4.2 Percent Suggested That the Economy May Be Gaining Momentum

Jeannine Aversa
Associated Press

WASHINGTON—The economy started out the year solidly, growing at an annual rate of 4.2 percent in the first quarter in a performance that suggests the recovery has staying power.

That is good news for President Bush, who is counting on healthy economic activity this summer as he campaigns for reelection.

The increase in gross domestic product from January through March was a slight improvement over the ?? rate over the final three months of last year, the Commerce Department reported Thursday.

The first quarterly report for 2004 fell short of the 5 percent pace analysts were forecasting. Nonetheless, it indicated the economy is on firm footing, economists said. Growth in the past three quarters has averaged 5.5 percent, the strongest for any similar period in 20 years.

"The economy has settled into a sustainable, self-reinforcing growth path," said Sung Won Sohn, chief economist at Wells Fargo.

GDP measures the value of all goods and services produced in the United States. It is considered the most important barometer of the economy's fitness. Spending by consumers, business and the federal government, especially on defense, contributed to first-quarter GDP.

The economy figures prominently in the presidential campaign between President Bush and presumptive Democratic nominee John Kerry.

"I have a sense that an economic light switch went on in the first quarter. Everyone is feeling so much more upbeat, and I think that will be reflected in the second-quarter GDP number," said Mark Zandi, chief economist at Economy.com.

From April through June, the economy is expected to expand at a rate in the range of 4.5 percent to 5 percent, according to some analysts. Growth in the second half of this year should clock in at around a 4 percent pace, some economists said.

"Looking forward, the prospects for sustaining solid economic growth in the period ahead are good," Federal Reserve Chairman Alan Greenspan told Congress last week.

In other economic news, the Labor Department reported that new filings for jobless benefits fell last week by 18,000 to 338,000, another sign that layoffs are easing. Also, the cost of workers' wages and benefits grew by 1.1 percent in the first quarter, the department said.

Federal Reserve policy-makers are expected to hold a key short-term interest rate at 1 percent, the lowest since 1958. Some economists believe the Fed will begin to raise rates later this year.

Greenspan: Soaring Budget Deficits Represent Long-Term Threat

WASHINGTON (AP)—America's soaring federal budget deficits represent a major obstacle to the country's long-term economic stability, Federal Reserve Chairman Alan Greenspan warned on Thursday.

Greenspan told a banking conference that the federal budget deficit was a bigger worry to him than America's soaring trade deficit or the high level of household debt because those two problems can be corrected by market forces.

"Our fiscal prospects are, in my judgment, a significant obstacle to long-term stability because the budget deficit is not readily subject to correction by market forces that stabilize other imbalances," he said in remarks to a banking conference.

Greenspan noted that the federal deficit, estimated to climb above $500 billion this year, will amount to 4.25% of the total economy after being in surplus just a few years ago.

He said one of the biggest concerns was that the deficits now were occurring right before the first wave of baby boomers will begin retiring.

"We have legislated commitments to our senior citizens that, given the inevitable retirement of our huge baby-boom generation, will create significant fiscal challenges in the years ahead," Greenspan said in his remarks, which were delivered by satellite to the conference in Chicago.

Greenspan cautioned that the country should not be lulled into a false sense of security about the federal deficit just because at the moment interest rates on long-term Treasury securities remain at low levels.

He said that the dollar's foreign exchange value has remained close to the average level of the past two decades in spite of soaring trade deficits and there have been no major economic disruptions triggered by record high household debt.

"Has something fundamental happened to the U.S. economy and, by extension, U.S. banking, that enables us to disregard all the time-tested criteria of imbalance and economic danger?" Greenspan asked.

Answering his own question, the Fed chairman said, "Regrettably, the answer is no. The free lunch has still to be invented."

Greenspan said he believed market forces would provide the impetus to move the trade deficit and high household debt to more sustainable levels.

But he said his concern was that there were no market forces that would push the country to deal with the federal budget deficit.

Greenspan did not offer a solution to the budget deficit in his speech Thursday although in the past he has called on Congress to move quickly to address the looming funding difficulties in Social Security by trimming the benefits of future retirees.

Two proposals he has suggested include raising the retirement age for receiving full Social Security benefits and reducing annual cost of living adjustments that Social Security recipients receive.

Federal Reserve policy-makers met on Tuesday and left a key interest rate at a 46-year low but signaled that they planned to start raising rates at a moderate pace in coming months, Greenspan did not address interest rates in his prepared remarks.

Glossary

Absolute advantage The ability to produce output with fewer resources than trading partners.

Aggregate demand curve Curve that relates aggregate demand to various price levels.

Average propensity to consume The fraction of consumption expenditure & disposable income.

Average propensity to save The fraction of savings & disposable income.

Business cycle Ups & downs in output of goods/services which impact employment & prices.

Comparative advantage The ability to produce output at least cost possible.

Cost-push inflation When price level increases because of the cost of one or more resources is higher, aggregate supply curve shifts to the left side.

Circular flow model The flow of goods/services/income among broad sectors of the economy.

Consumption function The invention of Mr. Keynes, C = a + b yd, which illustrates the relationship between consumption at different levels of income.

Cyclical unemployment Jobs seekers are more than the existing job vacancies found in the economy; it is caused by the deficiency in the aggregate demand curve.

Demand-pull inflation When price level increases because nation's demand for goods and services exceeds its ability to produce the goods/services at stable prices. The aggregate demand curve moves to the right of the aggregate supply curve reaching its vertical range. We have "too much money chasing too few goods."

Disposable income After-tax household income available for spending.

Equilibrium GDP Level of GDP when aggregate demand is equal to aggregate supply.

Expenditures approach A system for measuring GDP by summing up expenditures on final goods and services by households, businesses, governments, and net exports.

Federal Reserve System The U.S. central bank.

Frictional unemployment Unemployment due to normal shifts in turnover of people with skills.

Natural rate of full employment Acceptable employment level of 5%.

Income approach A system for measuring GDP by summing income.

Inflation An increase in the general price level.

Keynesian Theory A theory created by John M. Keyes, which introduces the consumption function, multiplier effect, and a different way to look at the savings/investment relationship.

M1 Cash (coins + paper currency) + checking.

Marginal propensity to consume Added consumption due to additional $1 more of disposable income.

Money Instrument universally accepted as medium of exchange for business transactions.

Nominal GDP The value of final goods and services, including current prices.

Okum's Law States that an annual 2-percent increase in real growth results in 1-percent decrease in the unemployment.

Open Market operations A tool of the Federal Reserve System to either increase or decrease the money supply.

Potential GDP The attainable GDP at 5% of unemployment.

Price index Changes in the general price level over time by comparing the cost of specified items.

Production possibilities curves Output produced by society using limited resources and available level of technology.

Real GDP The market value of final goods & services produced during a particular time frame, within a nation's borders.

Recession A decline in GDP that lasts for two consecutive quarters.

Reserve ratio Fraction that banks must keep at Federal Reserve Banks.

Structural unemployment Unemployment caused by changes in the structure of industry usually associated with technological changes.

Unemployment rate Percent of unemployed people divided by labor.